7 Steps to Succes Trading Options Online

BY LARRY D. SPEARS

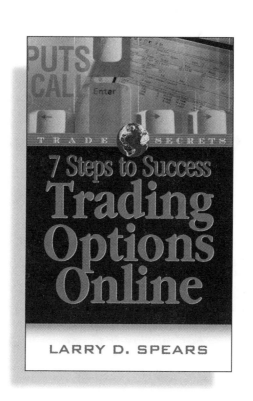

PUTS
CALL
Enter

T R A D E   SECRETS

7 Steps to Success
Trading
Options
Online

LARRY D. SPEARS

Titles in the
Trade Secrets Series

"Regardless of how much experience you may have had, if you haven't traded options online, then you haven't really traded options!"

— Larry D. Spears

ISBN 1-931611-25-4

Printed in the United States of America.

Contents

7 Steps
to Succes
Trading
Options
Online

Introduction

If You Haven't Traded Options Online, You Haven't Really Traded Options

Options are perhaps the most strategically versatile of all financial vehicles, with unique characteristics that give them a nearly universal appeal to investors. After all, what other vehicle can provide the promise of potentially limitless profits, yet require only a small initial cash outlay and, in most cases, offer precisely defined risks? That appeal is probably the primary reason you picked up this book in the first place. You *like* the option concept, and you'd *love* to be an active and artful trader—but you haven't quite figured out *how* to accomplish that goal.

Oh, sure, you've read up on the main option strategies—and even done a few option trades. Perhaps more than a few. Most modern stock investors have. And some of those trades have generated nice profits—certainly nice enough to keep your interest alive. But, in spite of their many advantages, options have yet to give you the overall results you'd like to achieve—the stellar success you *know* is possible. And you want to know *why!*

That's what this book is meant to explain. It's my contention, you see, that the majority of today's retail (non-professional) option investors fail to achieve their ultimate goals for one simple reason. No, it's not because of the specific options they choose to trade, nor is it due to the particular strategies they elect to use. While these issues are certainly important, I believe the major barrier blocking full success for most option investors is the cumbersome, inefficient and often costly process by which they actually trade.

To be more precise, if you're getting your research information, obtaining your price quotes and placing your option orders via telephone—talking one-on-one with a full-service (or even discount) stock broker—then you're not competing on a level playing field. Today's equity options market is fully computerized, ultra-fast paced and dominated by electronically plugged-in professional and institutional traders equipped with the latest research available on the companies they follow. If you're going to successfully play in such an arena, then you have to trade electronically, too. Otherwise, your data's too old, your actions are too slow and you are almost certainly paying fees that are too high. Thus, the only way you can hope to reap maximum option profits today is to instantly and directly access the markets through an online brokerage firm— preferably one that specializes in options.

If you've been trading options "the old-fashioned way" for very long, you may question the certainty with which I make that statement. However, given the impact computers and improved communications technologies have had on the financial markets over the past decade, I'll stand by it. In fact, just for emphasis, I'll even restate it in a slightly different way:

> Regardless of how much experience you may have had,
> if you haven't traded options online, then you haven't
> really traded options!

A Look Back Before Going Forward

To fully understand why I believe that statement—and why it's so important for you to consider online trading—you need to know a bit about why I'm qualified to make it. For starters, I *do* have a lot of experience. My trading career dates back to 1977, just four years after the Chicago Board Options Exchange first created and listed standardized equity options. I've tried every option strategy ever heard of (and several stinkers no one's heard of since)—profiting at times with most, and losing at others with all. I've burned countless gallons of midnight oil calculating stock volatility, figuring option valuations and working out strategy scenarios. I've written two other books on options trading, as well as four lessons on options in assorted home-study financial courses. In researching those manuscripts, I've interviewed dozens of brokers, floor traders, options specialists and other financial professionals—and, in reviewing reader reaction, I've heard scores of stories recounting both success and failure.

However, the most significant qualification I have for stressing the necessity of becoming an online trader is that I'm **NOT** an options professional—and never have been. Every options trade I've made has been as a retail customer, and all my options experience has been gained from a retail perspective. That's an important distinction, because most option books and advisory letters are written by professional traders—and they often provide a very distorted view of reality in the markets. They describe how transactions take place, how strategies work and the outstanding results they achieve with options—and all are colored by the benefits they receive as professionals, including quality research, instant pricing, priority executions and preferred commission rates. This creates unreasonable expectations and sets up many newer traders for failure, monetary loss and ultimate disillusionment with options. In truth, successfully trading options at the retail level isn't nearly as easy as it's commonly depicted—especially if you're doing it the old-fashioned way.

To illustrate, just consider my situation back in the mid-1980s—when the Internet still existed largely in the minds of a few government and university researchers, and the concept of trading anything "online" was the stuff of science fiction. At that time, I was an editor with *The Los Angeles Times*. I was also one of the most active options traders among the clients of a major full-service brokerage firm in downtown L.A.—and one of the most successful. I can assure you, however, that success wasn't easy.

To gauge my best opportunities and plan my strategies, I had to either work with the previous day's closing quotes from *The Wall Street Journal* or call my broker shortly after the market opening to see if new prices had been established. I then had to make a trading decision based on quick pencil work or gut instinct and call the broker again to place my order. If he'd gone into a meeting or to get coffee, I was stuck on hold as he was the only broker in the entire office who would take option orders. The others refused because they either felt options were too risky, making them inappropriate for their retail clients—a prejudice that unfortunately still persists among many brokers today—or because they simply didn't understand options well enough to risk personally dealing with them. My broker, being a trader himself, thus handled every option account the Los Angeles office carried.

An Obstacle Course to Execution

Once I'd given the order to my broker, the real challenge began. He phoned it in to the firm's central order desk, which wired it to the exchange where the particular option was listed (no cross-trading or multiple listing in those days). It was then written up by hand on an order slip and passed via a runner to the floor specialist in the proper area of the trading floor. Even though most of my orders involved the most actively traded options of the time—those on the S&P 100 Index, or OEX—there was still no guarantee of a rapid execution. Liquidity was typically thin for all but the nearest at-the-money contracts, so even market orders sometimes took several hours to fill. And, because bid/ask spreads were often outlandish—frequently as much as a dollar on a five- or six-dollar contract—I nearly always used a limit order, which slowed executions even further. As a result, split-price fills were common on market orders, and limit orders for as few as 10 or 20 contracts often came back incomplete or were filled in blocks. A good-till-canceled (GTC) order might even carry over until the next session—giving a whole new meaning to the expression "day trading."

The order's return trip was equally arduous, ending with a phone call from my broker verbally confirming the trade—a call that often didn't come until after the closing bell. This was a real drawback when the market or a target stock was making a big move, as I was sometimes eager to close a trade before I even knew for sure it had been opened.

Commissions were also a major barrier to success. Because I was an active trader, I got a preferred rate of $5 per contract, but the firm had a $50 "minimum ticket"—meaning one option cost the same as ten. And, if I received a split execution, I'd get dinged for dual commissions—$50 per ticket. As bad as that was, casual traders had it even worse, with their commissions being calculated based on trade value, as with stocks. Consequently, a two- or three-option trade might cost them as much as $120 to $150.

To be a successful options trader under such conditions, you had to be more than good—you had to be *very, very lucky*.

Of course, as time went on, the mechanics of trading got easier—but rather than helping, that actually served to widen the gap between retail and professional traders. By the early '90s, option liquidity had improved, the trading floors were becoming computerized, order processing was largely automated (meaning you got better, faster executions), and the boom in discount brokerages had driven down commission rates. Your broker's quote terminal could access option valuations, as well as screen for potentially advantageous trades. But, you still had to call to get the information—and place your orders by phone—meaning the pros who had full access to the electronic systems remained several steps ahead of retail traders. (Home quote systems and analytical software packages were available, but the costs—as much as $750 a month—made them impractical for most individuals.)

Changes in the marketplace also worked against non-professional traders. Volatility increased significantly as stocks rebounded following the crash of 1987 and mini-crash of '89 and moved into the long bull market. Option premiums soared, creating larger potential profits, but also altering some classic price relationships (e.g., in "calendar" or time spreads) and sharply increasing trading risks. Margin requirements were greatly expanded after the '87 debacle, making percentage returns on some strategies too small to justify the risks. Restraints were imposed on the size of market moves in an effort to control the impact of program trading, which sometimes left retail option investors locked out of the action. In addition, more and more new option products and contract variations, including serial expiration dates, were introduced. This broadened the opportunity set, but also made the analytical task almost overwhelming for the average investor.

In short, it got more and more difficult to be a successful retail options trader. Despite my experience and the diligence I applied to my trading, I increasingly felt I could no longer compete with the pros—and I had a growing number of losses to prove it. That's why, by the early '90s, my option-trading activity had dropped drastically. I wrote a few covered calls against stocks in my portfolio, and played an occasional longer-term, low-volatility spread —but did little else. And, because nothing occurred to ease the difficulties for retail traders, that personal attitude persisted—until just a couple of years ago.

The Restoration of Confidence

That's when the online brokerage industry—barely out of infancy itself—gave birth to the first programs allowing customers direct trading access to the options markets. Conceived in the combination of rapid growth in Internet usage, surging PC power levels, improving broadband communications technology, the full automation of exchange trading systems and swelling investor demand, those initial programs were far from perfect—but they held more than enough promise to rekindle my interest in active options trading. Now, with a steady stream of improvements, the regular addition of new features and more upgrades on the way, they have largely fulfilled that promise, becoming both efficient and versatile trading tools.

Complete details about the capabilities of the best online trading systems will be featured later, so I won't preview them in this Introduction. However, I will say that they truly are easy to use—and quite cost effective. As I noted earlier, when I was trading by phone with a full-service broker, it sometimes took me two days and three or four partial fills to complete a 20-contract position in even active index options—and costs could run as high as $25 per contract. Now, using my online account at PreferredTrade, Inc., in San Francisco, I can get a 20-contract market order filled instantly—even on a fairly thinly traded stock option—with commissions as low as $1.95 per contract. What's more, an order like that doesn't even represent a minor challenge for most online systems. For example, Michael Engmann, the founder and chairman of PreferredTrade, is a veteran options professional, but he now trades using the same online program as his company's customers—frequently doing more than a thousand trades a day.

That's certainly impressive, but it really doesn't reflect what I see as the prime achievement of the new online trading systems. That's the fact that they have fully restored my confidence as an options trader. Thanks to the online features now at my command, I'm convinced I can finally compete on an even footing with even the most savvy of the option pros—once again capturing the enormous profit potential these unique investment vehicles have to offer.

And, I'm equally convinced that—once you've taken "The Seven Key Steps to Success" outlined in the upcoming chapters—*you'll be able to do it, too!*

— **Larry D. Spears**

Chapter 1

KEY STEP NO. 1:
Learn How the Modern Electronic Option Markets Work

As should already be evident from the Introduction, the purpose of this book is twofold. First, we want to explain why, if you want to trade options, you really should be trading those options online. Secondly, we want to show you exactly how to do it—*and do it successfully*.

Our introductory descriptions of the difficulties and disadvantages involved in trading "the old-fashioned way" should have you steadfastly on course toward accepting the first premise, especially if you've experienced many of those same difficulties in your own past ventures into the options market. To accomplish our second goal, we've distilled the essential information into *seven key steps* —steps that we feel, when followed, should lead you clearly and directly to success in the world of online options trading.

As part of this distillation process, we have also made a couple of key assumptions. The first is that you are at least functionally knowledgeable about the basics of options. We will recap a few of the essential definitions in sidebar boxes along the way—but, for the most part, we'll assume you know the difference between, say, the exercise price and the premium. Our second assumption is that you already have a reasonably up-to-date personal or laptop computer, know what the Internet is and have the ability to get online via modem, DSL line, cable, satellite or other cyber science. Given that, apart from a few casual references, we won't discuss technology, equipment or software except insofar as it relates directly to conducting your online option trading activities.

That's not, of course, meant to diminish the importance of technology in the development of the modern electronic options markets. Absent the meteoric advances in computer and communications technology over the past two decades, trading options "online" wouldn't even be possible. Indeed, had someone used the term "online" in 1973, when standardized equity options were first introduced by the Chicago Board Options Exchange (CBOE), the assumption would have been that they were talking about transmitting orders via a Telex wire. And computers? No way! They were big, expensive and reserved for important things — certainly nothing so mundane as trading stocks or options. In fact, the initial process of trading options was largely manual. Orders went via phone or wire from the retail broker to his firm's central order desk, then on to the firm's trading desk at the designated exchange. There, order specifics were written on paper slips, which were carried by a runner to the appropriate pit and passed to the floor trader, who quickly reviewed them and then added his voice to a chorus of shouted bids and offers, negotiating via looks, nods and gestures until a deal was finally struck. Terms were then recorded and passed to the clearing agent, and the communications routing was reversed as news of the fill worked its way back to the customer — often taking several hours.

Today, the procedure works essentially the same, but now it's fully automated. Instead of trading pits, the floors of the stock and option exchanges are organized into clusters of computer terminals, with each cluster serving as the trading center for market makers handling a specific group of stocks or options. Overhead monitors display the current prices, most recent trades and the newest orders, nearly all of which are matched up electronically and quickly filled. In fact, at last count, the number of options trades being completed electronically had climbed *above 85 percent*. Floor traders, either representing brokerage firms or independents who make up what is known as "the trading crowd," do still negotiate larger or more complex orders, as well as those with desired prices "away from the market." The manual processing system is also maintained as a backup in case of electrical or computer-system problems.)

Where Your Trades Take Place:
The Leading Options Exchanges

Although more than 85 percent of option trades are now completed electronically, the leading option marketplaces in North America still have a physical presence and a distinct identity—the lone exception being the fledging International Securities Exchange, which is the nation's first completely electronic options market. Here is a brief overview of the five major option-trading arenas:

Chicago Board Options Exchange (CBOE) — As noted in the text, the CBOE was the originator of listed options trading in the United States, introducing a slate of standardized call options on just 16 underlying stocks in April 1973 (listed put options didn't come along until 1977). Today, the CBOE is the world's largest options exchange, listing options on more than 700 stocks, bonds and market indexes and boasting an average daily trading volume of more than 1.2 million contracts. The CBOE accounted for 45.8 percent of all U.S. option trades in 2000—a total of 312 million contracts. Ninety-four percent of those trades were completed electronically.

American Stock Exchange (AMEX) — The AMEX, based in New York, was organized to handle trading of stocks too small to be listed on the New York Stock Exchange. It expanded into options soon after the CBOE introduced listed contracts and now accounts for more than 27 percent of U.S. options trading volume. The AMEX allows trading in more than 1,400 different options, including those listed on all other major exchanges.

Pacific Exchange (PCX) — The Pacific Exchange in San Francisco is the third most active options exchange in the world, trading options on more than 800 individual stocks and a number of indexes (more than 1,800 stocks are also traded on the PCX). The PCX is a leader in electronic options trading, handling roughly 90 percent of its trades electronically—72 percent of which are processed automatically, with orders typically filled in under five seconds. The PCX accounted for nearly 16 percent of U.S. options volume in 2000.

Philadelphia Stock Exchange (PHLX) — The PHLX was America's first organized stock exchange, founded in 1790, and remains a highly active trading arena. More than 2,200 stocks, 920 equity options, 10 index options and 100 currency options trade on the PHLX, which handles around 8.5 percent of U.S. options volume.

International Securities Exchange (ISE) — As noted above, the ISE is the nation's first entirely electronic options market. Founded in 2000, the ISE is still in its infancy, accounting for less than 1 percent of U.S. options volume. However, the ISE's current plans call for listing and trading 600 stock options using 10 groups of market makers, each of which will handle trading in about 60 stock options via an interlinked computer network. The ISE will have no trading floor and no floor brokers, with all orders being processed electronically.

Note: Options are also traded on the Montreal Stock Exchange, the Toronto Stock Exchange and the Canadian Venture Exchange (formerly the Vancouver Exchange), but listings are primarily for Canadian stocks.

This electronic trading system, which is steadily being revised and upgraded as technologies improve, has allowed for an exponential increase in option-trading volume, as well as a phenomenal decline in the turnaround time for trades. Phone your broker with an order and he'll enter it electronically from his desk terminal, often getting return confirmation of a fill while you're still chatting—a far, far cry from the multi-hour waits described above. And even that seems slow when compared to the turnaround for an online trade. Place an online order to buy 10 July 25 Dell Computer calls "at the market," for example, and the entire order-entry and execution process occurs untouched by human hands—usually in 10 seconds or less. And you get instant confirmation of your trade, right on your home computer screen—as illustrated in Figure 1-1.

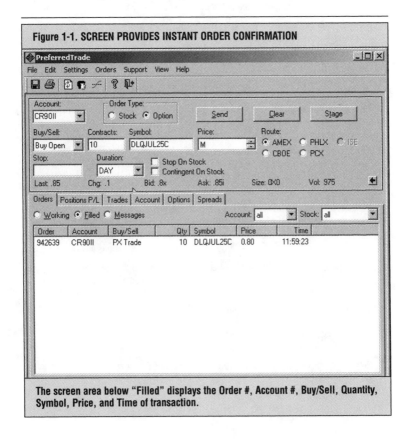

Figure 1-1. SCREEN PROVIDES INSTANT ORDER CONFIRMATION

The screen area below "Filled" displays the Order #, Account #, Buy/Sell, Quantity, Symbol, Price, and Time of transaction.

Lest you think it can't possibly be that easy, just consider that 72 percent of all option trades conducted last year on the Pacific Exchange—representing roughly 78 million contracts—were executed in precisely that fashion. And that percentage is growing annually—on every one of the nation's option exchanges. Obviously, not all those automatic fills came in response to online orders—but many millions did. And that number is also growing rapidly every year.

The key to that growth, of course, is increased acceptance and use of the Internet by retail investors.

The Internet Opens Up Markets to 'The Little Guy'

Technology, as represented by computers and dedicated communications networks, actually began to impact the financial markets in the late 1960s. By the mid-'70s, computers were being widely used by the research, accounting and back-office divisions of most brokerage firms, and automation was rapidly beginning to infiltrate the exchange floors. And, by the mid-'80s, virtually every professional in the investment business—from broker to fund manager, from analyst to arbitrageur—was "wired," able to monitor the latest news, access the latest research, crunch the latest numbers and communicate orders directly to the trading floor. The poor retail investor, however, was lagging far behind. Oh, sure, PCs were beginning to pop up on the desks of quite a few investors, as was analytical software, both fundamental and technical, that could be used on them. But those programs were costly and slow, and financial data was hard to come by—and even more expensive. As for the idea of having your home computer directly dial the stock exchange and place an order, that was unheard of. However, the Internet was about to change all that.

Although conceived in 1969 by computer specialists with the Department of Defense as a means of exchanging information, the Internet really didn't become widely accessible to the public until 1989. That's when the World-Wide Web debuted, allowing computer-to-computer transfer of not only text, but graphics and sound as well. Even then, usage grew relatively slowly. It wasn't until late 1995 that the Internet boom finally started, ignited by the synergy of lower computer prices, advanced processor capabilities and improved telecommunications technologies. The resulting shock wave swept 'round the globe, enveloping more than 420 million people by mid-2001. As part of that Internet expansion, the number of online stock traders also exploded, with the roster of cyberinvestors now projected to reach 20.3 million by 2003—representing *$3 trillion in annual trading volume*.

With that kind of market potential, not to mention their own savings from internal efficiencies and lower costs, it's no wonder leading stock and option exchanges moved so quickly to develop systems to facilitate online trading—nor is it a surprise that so many new brokerage firms were created to cater to it.

Key Elements of the Electronic Trading System

We won't attempt to give precise credit for the many innovations that have led to the current state of online options trading, simply because they have come from many sources. Each of the exchanges has made contributions, either directly or through contractors, as have technicians at a number of brokerage firms, computer manufacturers and other technology-related companies. Besides, you don't need that information. All you really care about, as a potential online options trader, is that the electronic trading systems of the exchanges work reliably, accurately and in easy conjunction with your broker's order-entry software. Still, to be successful, you should have at least a basic understanding of how the system functions, so let's look at a brief overview.

At the heart of today's electronic markets are the automatic order-routing and trade-execution systems employed by each of the option exchanges. Although they have different names and a few subtle differences, these systems function in essentially the same fashion—based on one fundamental rule that all market makers and exchange members must abide by. It states: "Orders that meet specified parameters are *guaranteed* a fill at the current market bid or offer."

This concept was developed by the CBOE as the basis for its Retail Automatic Execution System (RAES), which was designed to standardize electronic order execution procedures and give retail customers the fastest fills possible. Without exaggeration, implementation of the RAES system literally revolutionized trading on the CBOE floor, and the other option exchanges followed suit as soon as they could get the technology in place. The other automated-execution systems are known as AMOS at the American Stock Exchange, POETS at the Pacific Exchange, AUTOM at the Philadelphia Exchange and ISE at the International Securities Exchange.

To ensure that the process functions in an orderly fashion during each trading session — and that responsibility for the "guaranteed" trades is shared equally among all exchange participants — market makers and floor traders must "sign on" to the electronic system each day. Then, when trading begins, the system randomly selects a market maker and assigns the first automatic trade to him. All subsequent executions are then assigned in order, based on an alphabetic or numeric code sequence.

In order to qualify for a guaranteed execution under RAES or one of the other systems, an option order must generally be for 20 con-

The Public Order Book — and OPRA

The "public order book" is an electronic cueing system maintained by each exchange to sort and prioritize open customer orders that aren't eligible for automatic execution. These can include orders placed prior to the market opening, limit orders with prices away from the market, good-till-canceled orders, orders too large for existing liquidity and orders that exceed the automatic-execution limits. These orders are monitored by floor brokers and the trading crowd, looking for incoming orders with which to match them, as well as for moves by the market that would make them eligible for automatic execution. If such a move occurs, they are rerouted to the automated system and given priority over any identical, but newer orders.

Regardless of how or where an option order is executed, the electronic trading system does two things as soon as the transaction is completed. The first is to send a "fill report," or confirmation, to the customer (via the broker, or through the broker's direct-entry order system for online traders). The second is to send the sale information to the Options Price Reporting Authority, or OPRA, which instantaneously transmits the last-price data to quote systems worldwide. That's how traders monitoring streaming quote systems at the Pacific Exchange in California can know the exact price for an option that last traded on the AMEX in New York — and vice versa.

tracts or less, although this limit is expanded to 50 for some index options. The order must be a "market" order or a limit order at the "bid" (for sales) or the "offer" (for purchases). The option itself must be in one of the three most actively traded expiration series, and the option premium must be $10 or under.

If an order meets those criteria, there are only two circumstances under which the guaranteed execution won't be carried out on a given exchange. The first is if a better price is available on another exchange where the option also trades. (U.S. options exchanges all belong to an Electronic Communications Network, or ECN, that enables the latest sales prices, bids and offers for a given option to be displayed on all floor terminals where that option is traded, regardless of the exchange at which they are located.) In that case, the order will be routed to the "public order book," where it will generally be executed by a member of the trading crowd.

The second circumstance when an order won't be automatically executed is when an identical order is already on the public order book and has not yet been filled. In that case, the newer order is rerouted to another execution system, where it falls in behind the older order that was already on the books.

The advent of guaranteed automatic execution has obviously been of great benefit to smaller retail options traders, putting them on exactly the same footing as larger institutional traders. It's a far cry

---

The "Unbundling" Rule

If you don't believe the automatic-execution systems give you an edge over professional options traders, you should be aware that Securities and Exchange Commission (SEC) rules specifically prohibit registered broker/dealers and their associates from using the systems to execute institutional trades. The exchanges also have rules barring broker/dealers from splitting—or "unbundling"—large orders into quantities of 20 contracts or less in order to qualify for the system, and the computers monitor account designations to assure compliance. In fairness, retail customers are also discouraged from "unbundling" their larger orders. Some brokers even build brief order-entry delays into their software so they can monitor for essentially identical small orders coming back-to-back out of the same account. All this because the automatic execution system is such an efficient and cost-effective way to trade options.

---

from the old days, when small retail orders routinely got placed at the bottom of the stack and filled only after the floor trader had satisfied the needs of his major players. It's also one of the primary reasons why, if you're going to trade options, you really should be trading online, where you can maximize the advantages gained through instant execution.

What If You Don't Qualify?

If you're a typical retail trader, the bulk of your individual orders will probably qualify for automatic execution—though we can certainly hope many of your trades will prove so successful you'll be closing long-option positions at prices well above the $10 limit. Assuming that's the case, here's how those orders will typically be handled.

For starters, even though execution of your order won't be guaranteed, it will almost certainly still be handled electronically, with a fill occurring in a matter of minutes (assuming your requested price is near the market bid or offer). As noted earlier, the exchanges all have similar systems for electronic handling of orders, but for ease of explanation, let's assume your order went to the CBOE, which is where nearly half of all option trades take place. When the order hits the CBOE and fails to qualify for RAES execution, it will be assigned to the exchange's Public Automated Routing (PAR) system, the computerized trading network used by CBOE floor brokers.

The first stop within the PAR system is the computer workstation of your brokerage firm's floor trader, where it is slotted in with the firm's other "working" (or pending) orders. Using a feature of the system called the "Deck Manager," the firm's floor broker can automatically sort orders, viewing all orders for an entire class on a single screen. The broker is also able to see the best current bid and offer for each option series, as well as for his clients' specific orders. Entries on this screen are color coded to alert the broker where the orders he's working are priced, relative to the current market quote.

The firm's floor broker has several alternatives regarding how to deal with a specific order. The first is to try to match the order with another from the firm's own order book, providing what is in effect an in-house execution. The second—usually chosen when trading is very heavy and the broker can't adequately work the order—is to send the order to the public order book (known as the EBOOK at the CBOE), where it is cued up for execution as soon as the market moves enough to meet the specific terms of the order. The final, and most likely, alternative is that the order will be actively worked among the trading crowd.

To do this, the firm's broker simply highlights the order, touches the "Crowd" key on his terminal and PAR routes the order to the workstation of a floor broker in the group of traders that routinely deal in options for the specified underlying stock or index. That "crowd broker" then routes the order to the hand-held terminals of every floor trader who buys and sells that particular option—one (or more) or whom usually accepts the terms and executes the order. Details of the fill (price, size and opposing buyer or seller) are then routed back to the initiating broker, who completes an "electronic trading card" that was created when the order first came in, then confirms the trade to the customer and sends the price information to OPRA.

The importance of the hand-held terminals should be emphasized, as they are another of the innovations that have made online option trading a reality. Nifty little devices weighing just over a pound, they have eliminated the need for paper order slips and floor runners, allowing instant and simultaneous distribution of orders to every possible buyer or seller—and equally fast return notification of order acceptance and execution. They are now used by virtually every floor trader and market maker at the CBOE (and other exchanges), with more than 1,300 hand-held units currently linked to RAES, PAR and the other electronic order-routing systems. That explains why the CBOE is able to boast that fully 94 percent of all public customer orders are now executed electronically.

It should also be noted that, with only a few exceptions, it takes less time for a market order to go through the full execution process just described, than it took for you to read the descriptions. Obviously, execution times increase as the price constraints get more restrictive, the size gets larger or the orders get more complex, but nearly all are still far faster—and far less costly—than they were even 10 years ago.

Step 1 Is Complete

You've now seen a fairly complete overview of how the modern electronic option markets work—and how they work to greatly increase your competitiveness as a retail options trader. There is one other key electronic component of the online trading process —your personal broker's order-entry system and software package—but we'll save our discussion of that until Step No. 7, when we talk about choosing the right online broker. For now, let's move on to Key Step No. 2 and review the most effective options strategies for use in your online trading program.

Chapter 2

KEY STEP NO. 2:
Utilize the Most Effective Trading Strategies

As already acknowledged, options are among the most versatile of investment vehicles. They can be used for the most aggressive of speculations—and for purely defensive purposes. They can be used to produce large one-time profits—or to generate a steady stream of income. They can be used in the riskiest of investment pursuits—or to specifically insure against risk. They can be used when markets rise, when they fall—or when they fail to move at all. They can be used by themselves, in conjunction with other options of the same or different type, in combination with their underlying securities—even with groups of essentially unrelated stocks.

Indeed, there are at least two-dozen distinct investment strategies using options alone—and half again as many using options in association with other securities. And, although it may take some thought and timing, virtually all of these strategies can be implemented online. Clearly, in a book of this size, space won't allow us to cover them all—or even the majority. However, in this Key Step, we will look at some of the most effective option strategies and discuss the best way to position them through your online trading account. Along the way, we'll also review a few of the basics regarding options and their characteristics, just in case it's been a while since you've traded.

Goals Determine Choice of Strategies

Obviously, the strategies you employ in your online trading will be dictated by the goals you hope to achieve using options. If you expect a major market move and your desire is to reap maximum speculative profits, then you'll likely pick the simplest and most direct of the option strategies—the outright purchase of a put or call, depending on your views about the direction of the move. If you expect a more modest price move, but still want to seek speculative profits, then you might take a more conservative approach, choosing a vertical spread using either puts or calls, again depending on whether you are bullish or bearish. If you expect a major price move but aren't sure about the direction, you may opt to

---

Options Defined

Whether the underlying instruments are stocks, indexes, currencies or even commodity futures, there is one absolute regarding options—there are only two basic types (or classes). They are:

CALLS—A call option gives its owner the right to **BUY** the underlying security at a specific price for a limited period of time. In the case of equity options, the purchaser of a call receives the right to buy 100 shares of the underlying stock at the option's stated strike price. As a rule, purchasers of call options are bullish, expecting the price of the underlying stock to rise during the period leading up to the option's specified expiration date. Conversely, sellers of calls are usually bearish, expecting the price of the underlying stock to fall—or, at the least, remain stable—prior to the option's expiration. There may, however, be other reasons for selling calls, including the structuring of strategies such as spreads.

PUTS—A put option gives its owner the right to **SELL** the underlying security at a set price for a limited period of time. With equity options, the purchaser of a put receives the right to sell 100 shares of the underlying stock at the option's specified strike price. Buyers of put options are generally bearish, expecting the price of the underlying stock to fall prior to the option's stated expiration date. Conversely, sellers of puts are usually bullish, expecting the price of the underlying stock to rise—or at least remain stable—through the option's expiration date. There may, however, be other reasons for selling puts related to the objectives of certain strategies, such as lowering the cost basis on an intended eventual purchase of the underlying stock.

Options also come in two different styles, based on when they can be exercised. **American-style options** can be exercised *at any time* prior to the stated expiration date, whereas **European-style options** can be exercised *only at the time of expiration.* With the exception of a few options tied to major market indexes, all options currently traded in North America are American-style.

---

position one of the more exotic "delta neutral" strategies, such as a straddle or "strangle." If you own a stock and need to generate more income from your holdings, you might add an option to the mix and write a covered call. Or, if you own a large selection of stocks and want to protect yourself against a market downturn, you could choose to buy puts on a broad-based stock index.

In short, the strategic possibilities—like the potential profits offered by options—are virtually unlimited. Whatever your specific goal, you can probably find a way to achieve it using options—assuming, of course, that you are correct in your assessment of what the market (or a given stock) is going to do, and that you structure your option strategy properly. We can't do much to ensure you are correct in evaluating the market—beyond perhaps urging diligence in your research and economic monitoring. However, we can show you when and how to implement some of the key option strategies—so we will.

The Strategic Starting Point—Buying an Option

The most basic use of an option is as a purely speculative vehicle. In fact, a recent market study found that 68 percent of all option trades during a five-year period involved the simple speculative purchase of a put or call. (Call buyers accounted for roughly 70 percent of that total, a function of the inherent tendency for investor optimism.) The reasoning behind this statistic is easy to understand. When you buy an option, your initial cost is low—far lower than if you traded the stock underlying the option. In addition, your risk is strictly limited to the amount you pay for the option. However, your actual dollar profit potential, which is unlimited, can be almost as large as with the actual stock—and your percentage return on a successful trade can be 10, 20 or even 30 times larger.

Thus, it's no wonder that buying options is such a popular speculative strategy. Unfortunately, it's also one of the least successful—with some studies putting the number of losing trades above 90 percent. Once again, however, that represents a weakness in the option buyer's market analysis or timing, not a flaw in the strategy. And, so there won't be any flaws in your strategy when you

The Elements of an Option

There are certain terms unique to options—terms that primarily describe the specifics of each individual option contract. In order to define these terms, let's assume you just bought an "October 120 IBM call option at a price of $4.50 per share."

- **The underlying stock (or index)**—This is the security the option gives you the right to buy or sell. In this case, 100 shares of IBM common stock.

- **The strike price (also called exercise price)**—This is the guaranteed price at which you can "exercise" your option—in other words, at which you can buy or sell the underlying stock. In this case, the price at which you can buy 100 shares of IBM stock is $120 per share.

- **The expiration date**—This is the date on which your option expires—in other words, the date after which you can no longer buy or sell the underlying stock at the strike price. Options on stocks in the U.S. officially expire on "the Saturday following the third Friday of the expiration month" (although trading stops at the market close on the third Friday). Thus, this IBM call would expire on the third Saturday in October.

- **The premium**—The premium is simply the price you pay to buy an option, quoted on a per-share basis. (The seller of an option gets to keep the premium, regardless of whether the option is ever exercised or not.) In this case, the premium was $4.50 per share—or $450 for the entire 100-share option contract.

buy a call or put online, we'll summarize the risk parameters for each in the tables below, then walk through an actual example. (*Note: For consistency and ease of explanation, all strategy assessments and examples will be based on standard American-style equity options, with the underlying asset being 100 shares of common stock rather than a market index or other security. In addition, please check with your individual brokerage firm for its exact margin requirements and trading policies. These can differ from firm to firm.*)

Strategy 1—Going Long a Call

Trade Description: Purchase a call option.
Expectation: The price of the underlying stock will *rise* substantially prior to the option's expiration date.
Break-Even Point: The striking price, plus the premium paid for the call.

Potential Profit: Unlimited, once the price of the underlying stock rises above the break-even point.

Maximum Risk: Limited to the premium initially paid for the call.

Cost to Open: The premium paid for the call, plus commission.

Margin Requirement: The full purchase price of the call.

Strategy 2—Going Long a Put

Trade Description: Purchase a put option.

Expectation: The price of the underlying stock will *fall* substantially prior to the option's expiration date.

Break-even Point: The striking price, minus the premium paid for the put.

Potential Profit: Unlimited, once the price of the underlying stock goes below the break-even point (except to the extent the stock price could fall to zero).

A Word on Margin Requirements

Because certain option strategies — such as the "naked" sale of a call or put — can carry risks far in excess of the actual cash required to initiate them, the option exchanges mandate that traders doing these strategies deposit cash (or securities) with their brokerage firms as collateral to guarantee they will meet the obligations imposed by the strategies. This collateral — referred to as a "margin requirement" or "margin deposit" — varies from strategy to strategy, based on the option exchange's assessment of the position's relative risk, and must remain on deposit for the duration of the trade. If brokerage firms feel the relative risk is higher than that perceived by the exchange, they may demand that clients make a larger deposit; however, no brokerage firm may require less than the "exchange minimum." Should the market move against a trader holding such a position, causing a loss, he or she may receive a "margin call" requiring the deposit of additional funds to bring the collateral up to the "maintenance level." Failure to meet such a call could result in the forced closure of the margined position.

The actual formulas for calculating margin requirements are quite complex, so we won't try to explain them here. However, your broker's computer should calculate them automatically and inform you immediately if you have insufficient equity in your account to secure a new option position. The need to ensure that you have enough money available to meet potential margin requirements is the primary reason most brokerage firms require a minimum deposit of $5,000 to $10,000 to open an account — even though the individual options you want to buy may only cost $300 or $400.

Maximum Risk: Limited to the premium initially paid for the put.
Cost to Open: The premium paid for the put, plus commission.
Margin Requirement: The full purchase price of the put.

As noted earlier, the simple purchase of a put or call is the essence of option trading. Not only does a long option position give you the biggest bang for your speculative buck, but it also provides the foundation for structuring virtually every combination play, regardless of your ultimate goal. Fortunately, it's also the easiest strategy to understand—and the most effortless to place using your online broker's order-entry system. To prove it, let's walk through an example—from inspiration to execution.

Let's Trade — Buying a Cisco Call

Assume you've been monitoring several stocks in the technology sector, which has been beaten down, but which you feel is ready for a rebound. You particularly like the outlook for Cisco Systems, Inc., believing it could beat second-quarter earnings estimates based on a surge in new orders. Those earnings will be reported during the second week in July, and you think that could spark a strong rally in Cisco's stock price—just before expiration of the July options.

So, on an early June morning, just after the market opening, you log onto the Internet, click on the icon for your broker's online trading program, wait a few seconds for it to load, type in your user name and password and access your account—all in under a minute. Using the quote-retrieval feature of the order-entry program, you type in Cisco's stock symbol, CSCO, click the "request" button and, in about four seconds, find that Cisco just traded at $19.35 a share. That seems like an attractive price—especially since you think the stock could be above $25 a share by mid-July—so you briefly ponder purchasing the actual stock. It would cost you $1,935 to buy 100 shares and a move to $25 would make your position worth $2,500, giving you a profit of $565 (less commissions of about $30)—and a return of 27.6 percent. Not half bad for a seven-week trade!

But wait a minute! This book's about trading options online, so you don't really want to buy the stock. You just considered it for the sake of comparison. What you really did, after finding that Cisco stock was priced at $19.35, was click the "option quotes" flag on the program screen and request quotes for all the July Cisco options with strike prices close to the current stock price. Five seconds later, the following grid, Figure 2-1, appears and you begin your search for the right option. (*Note: In reality, you'll probably trade in larger lots than one, but for the sake of clarity, consistency and ease of calculation, our examples will assume purchase of one contract or one set of options unless otherwise noted.*)

FIGURE 2-1.   CISCO SYSTEMS OPTION PRICE QUOTES
LAST: **19.35** CHG: .35 BID: **19.34** ASK: **19.35** VOL: **521384**

CALLS							SYMBOL	PUTS						
LAST	HIGH	LOW	VOL	OPRA	BID	ASK		BID	ASK	OPRA	HIGH	LOW	VOL	LAST
5.00	5.20	4.80	642	GC	4.80	4.90	CYQJUL15	.50	.55	SC	.55	.45	96	.50
3.00	3.40	2.95	381	GW	3.00	3.10	CYQJUL17.5	1.10	1.20	SW	1.25	1.00	2349	1.15
1.75	2.00	1.55	3659	GD	1.75	1.80	CYQJUL20	2.25	2.35	SD	2.50	2.10	1873	2.40
.85	1.00	.80	1928	GX	.80	.90	CYQJUL22.5	3.90	4.10	SX	4.10	3.60	724	3.90
.40	.50	.35	1050	GE	.40	.45	CYQJUL25	5.90	6.10	SE	6.10	5.80	228	6.00

Table and prices provided by PreferredTrade, Inc.

You first look at the prices for the July $17.50 call, shown on the second line of the right side of the grid, and see that it's priced at $3.00 bid/$3.10 ask. However, that call is nearly $2.00 in the money —which would make it a fairly conservative pick for a play as aggressively bullish as you want to make. Besides, with a premium of $3.10, it would cost you $310 per option—all of which you'd lose if you turned out to be wrong. That's a little more than you want to risk on this speculation. So, you turn to the slightly out-of-the-money July 20 call.

With an ask price of $1.80, the July 20 Cisco call would cost $180 (plus commission), which is not an unreasonable price for an at-the-money option with seven weeks of life left—particularly on a stock as historically volatile as Cisco. (From 1996 to early 2000, when the high-techs were hyper-hot, a similarly positioned Cisco call would have been priced at $6.50 or $7.00.) The biggest negative for this call is that it will expire worthless, giving you a total loss, unless Cisco stock climbs at least 66 cents to $20.01 per share. You'll also need a move to $21.80 in order to break even (before commission charges). However, if Cisco stock does rise to $25 a

In, At or Out of the Money

Perhaps the most important component of an option's premium is the position of its strike price relative to the actual price of the underlying stock. All options are either *in the money* or *out of the money* at any given time—except for the rare occasion when the stock price is *exactly* the same as the option's strike price. And, because many strategies call for buying or selling in-the-money or out-of-the-money options—or both—it is important to know which is which. By definition, an in-the-money option is one that has *real*—or *intrinsic*—value, while an out-of-the-money option is one that has only time value. There is, however, an easier way to make the distinction:

> **CALLS** with strike prices **below** the actual stock price are **in the money**.
> **CALLS** with strike prices **above** the actual stock price are **out of the money**.
> **PUTS** with strike prices **above** the actual stock price are **in the money**.
> **PUTS** with strike prices **below** the actual stock price are **out of the money**.

Traditionally, the put or call with the strike price closest to the actual stock price—whether slightly in the money or slightly out of the money—is referred to as being at the money.

The choice of option strike price, relative to the underlying stock price, is a significant consideration when deciding exactly how speculative you want to be in buying options, as explained below:

CONSERVATIVE—As a rule, the purchase of the *in-the-money option* represents the most modest speculation. Although it carries the largest premium, and is therefore most expensive, the in-the-money option is actually less risky because it requires the smallest stock price move to reach the break-even point and begin producing a profit. The stock also must make a sizeable move against you—enough to carry the option out of the money—before you suffer a total loss. On comparably sized price moves, real-dollar profits are larger on in-the-money options than on at- or out-of-the-money options. However, because of the higher cost, the percentage return on a profitable trade is usually lower.

MODERATE—The *at-the-money option* purchase provides the most balanced speculative play. The cost, and therefore the maximum risk, is moderate—as is the size of the stock-price move required to reach the break-even point and begin producing a profit. However, any adverse price move—or even a stable market—will typically result in the option expiring worthless, giving you a total loss. Dollar profits generally aren't as large, but percentage returns are higher than with in-the-money options.

AGGRESSIVE—The most blatant speculative purchase utilizes the *out-of-the-money option*. Although the premium, and thus the real-dollar risk, is low, the stock can move almost a full strike-price level in your favor—and you'll still suffer a total loss. And, an even larger move is needed before the trade starts making a profit. But, because of the small dollar outlay, when you do get one right, the percentage returns are truly spectacular.

share, as you expect, the July 20 call will be worth $5.00—and you'll have a profit of $320 on your trade (less commissions). Even after subtracting commissions of about $40, you'll still be looking at *a return of more than 155 percent!*

Thus, though your real-dollar gain would be less than with a direct purchase of the stock, *your return would be almost six times larger!* That's an ideal illustration of the kind of leverage routinely offered by options—and a perfect explanation of why they are so popular. Plus, if you ignore the one-contract constraint of our example and use the entire $1,935 you'd have spent on 100 shares of stock to buy calls, you'd get 10 contracts—meaning your dollar gain on the trade would be $3,200 (less the very same $40 in commissions).

Since that's the kind of scenario you like in your "moderate" speculations, you decide to go ahead with the purchase of a July 20 Cisco call. You move your cursor back to the order-entry portion of the screen, click "Option" under "Order Type," designate the order as a "Buy Open," enter the symbol (Cisco's option symbol is CYQ) and your desired price, and then click send. The broker's computer (at least if you're using my broker, PreferredTrade) then scans quotes at all the option exchanges—in this instance routing it to the Pacific Exchange (PCX), where it found the best price (in a minor miracle, actually a nickel lower at $1.75), as shown in Figure 2-2. Because that's the market price and the order is for less

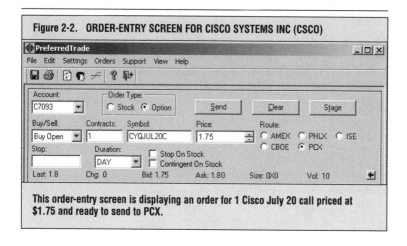

Figure 2-2. ORDER-ENTRY SCREEN FOR CISCO SYSTEMS INC (CSCO)

This order-entry screen is displaying an order for 1 Cisco July 20 call priced at $1.75 and ready to send to PCX.

than 20 contracts, the Pacific's POETS system automatically executes the trade, and a confirmation shows up on the "filled orders" section of your screen—most likely in less than 20 seconds.

That's how this most basic of option strategies is positioned, how well it might work if you prove right about the market—and how easy it is to actually initiate your trades when you do your analysis and enter your orders online.

The process of choosing an underlying stock, evaluating the related options, making a trading decision and actually executing the trade online works exactly the same with puts as with calls—except, of course, your expectations for the stock-price movement are bearish. Given that, we won't walk through a specific example of a put purchase—nor will we provide examples of selling a call or put short. While the motivations in using those strategies are substantially different and the risk/reward characteristics are reversed, actual execution of the trades is nearly identical. You merely designated the order as an "Open Sell" transaction. For those not familiar with the risks, however, the following tables detail the specifics of the basic "short" option positions.

Strategy 3—Selling a Call Short

Trade Description: Sell a call option.

Expectation: The price of the underlying stock will *fall* below the strike price prior to the option's expiration date and the call will thus expire worthless.

Break-Even Point: The striking price, plus the premium received for the call.

Potential Profit: Limited to the premium received at the time the call is sold.

Maximum Risk: Unlimited, once the stock rises above the break-even point.

Cost to Open: Commission only, but premium received must stay in account.

Margin Requirement: 100% of option proceeds, plus 20% of the underlying security, less the out-of-the-money amount, subject to a minimum of 10% of the value of the underlying security. Some brokers may have higher margin requirements.

Strategy 4 — Selling a Put Short

Trade Description: Sell a put option.

Expectation: The price of the underlying stock will *rise* above the strike price prior to the option's expiration date and the put will thus expire worthless. As an alternate strategy, some investors sell puts in hopes the stock price will fall below the strike price. This will give them the opportunity to buy the shares at a price below current market value, and also have their cost basis further reduced by the premium received for the put.

Break-Even Point: The striking price, minus the premium received for the put.

Potential Profit: Limited to the premium received at the time the put is sold.

Maximum Risk: Unlimited, once the stock falls below the break-even point.

Cost to Open: Commission only, but premium received must stay in account.

Margin Requirement: 100% of option proceeds, plus 20% of the underlying security, less the out-of-the-money amount, subject to a minimum of 10% of the value of the underlying security. Some brokers may have higher margin requirements.

Vertical Spreads — A More Modest Speculation

Many investors like the idea of taking speculative profits from the options market, but don't like the high failure rate associated with merely buying calls or puts. They also don't feel comfortable trying to predict stock-price moves of the size typically needed to make those solo option strategies profitable. For these investors, a popular — and extremely effective — speculative alternative is the vertical option spread. And, thanks to recent upgrades in order-processing technology, you can now initiate and close out these highly useful strategies just as easily online as through a regular broker.

Vertical spreads can be done with either puts or calls — depending on your market orientation — and have numerous advantages over an outright option purchase. These benefits frequently (though not always) include a lower initial cost, smaller dollar risk, less dramatic swings in position value, closer break-even points and a higher overall rate of success. And what do you have to give up to obtain the added edge these spreads offer? Essentially, just one thing—the opportunity for unlimited profits.

How a Spread Is Structured

Although it involves two options, rather than one, structuring a vertical spread is relatively simple. It involves buying one option and simultaneously selling another of the same type and expiration date, but with a different strike price. The difference, or spread, between the two strike prices—in combination with the debit (or credit) created by offsetting the two option premiums—establishes both a maximum loss and a maximum profit for the trade. And, the position of the two strike prices relative to the current price of the underlying stock determines the relative aggressiveness of the speculation.

There are four basic kinds of vertical spreads. The two most popular—a **bullish** spread, done with **calls** and a **bearish** spread, done with **puts**—are referred to as **debit spreads** because you pay more for the option you buy than you receive for the option you sell, thereby creating **an opening debit**. The other two, a **bearish** spread done with **calls** and a **bullish** spread done with **puts**, are called **credit spreads** because you receive a larger premium for the option you sell than you pay for the option buy, thereby generating **an opening credit**. The risk/reward parameters for the two debit spreads are outlined below. Review them— and the actual trading example that follows—after which we'll provide similar risk/reward assessments for the two credit spreads.

Strategy 5—A Bullish Vertical Call Spread

Trade Description: Buy a call option, typically either in or at the money, and simultaneously sell another call option on the same underlying stock and with the same expiration date, but with a *higher* strike price.

Expectation: The price of the underlying stock will *rise* above the strike price of the call sold prior to the option's expiration date, thereby generating a profit equal to the difference between the two strike prices, minus the debit paid to open the position.

Break-even Point: The strike price of the call purchased, plus the per-share debit paid to open the trade.

Potential Profit: Limited to the difference between the strike prices of the two calls involved, less the debit paid to establish the position.

Maximum Risk: Limited to the debit paid to initiate the spread (the per-share debit x 100 x number of contracts).

Cost to Open: The amount of the opening debit, plus commissions.

Margin Requirement: Typically none because the long call "covers" the short call. However, some brokers require a minimum margin ($250 to $500) on all option short sales, even those done as part of a limited-risk spread. (This provides some protection for the firm should the trader later decide to "leg out" of the spread by selling the long call, leaving him or her short a "naked" call.)

Strategy 6 — A Bearish Vertical Put Spread

Trade Description: Buy a put option, typically either in or at the money, and simultaneously sell another put option on the same underlying stock and with the same expiration date, but with a *lower* strike price.

Expectation: The price of the underlying stock will *fall* below the strike price of the short put prior to the expiration date, thereby generating a profit equal to the difference between the two strike prices, minus the opening debit.

Break-Even Point: The strike price of the put purchased, minus the per-share debit paid to open the position.

Potential Profit: Limited to the difference between the strike prices of the two puts involved, less the opening debit.

Maximum Risk: Limited to the debit paid to initiate the trade (the per-share debit x 100 x number of contracts).

Cost to Open: The amount of the opening debit, plus commissions.

Margin Requirement: None, because the long put "covers" the short put, subject to the discretion of your individual brokerage firm, which may require a minimum margin ($250 to $500) on any option short sale.

Driving to Profits — A Sample GM Spread

Now that you've seen those strategy profiles, let's look at an actual example. Assume it's early June and you're expecting a modest summer rally among the Blue Chips, led by the automotive issues, whose sales have started to benefit from an earlier series of interest-rate cuts by the Federal Reserve. You particularly like the outlook for General Motors, which is currently trading around $56 a share. You feel it could easily climb above $60 by mid-July, but you really don't want to put up the $5,600-plus it would cost to buy a 100-share round lot. Besides, while a $400 profit on a $5,600 investment in less than two months isn't bad (a 7.1 percent return), it isn't really spectacular either. So, you decide to play the expected GM move using options.

A check of your broker's online order screen quickly shows that GM common's last trade was at $56.05, unchanged on the day, and the current ask price is $56.10. Not quite sure what strategy you want to employ, you ask for quotes on all July GM options with strike prices between 45 and 65 — and the following grid, Figure 2-3, pops up on your screen:

FIGURE 2-3.   GENERAL MOTORS OPTION PRICE QUOTES
LAST: **56.05** CHG: **.00** BID: **56.05** ASK: **56.10** VOL: **40856**

CALLS							SYMBOL	PUTS						
LAST	HIGH	LOW	VOL	OPRA	BID	ASK	SYMBOL	BID	ASK	OPRA	HIGH	LOW	VOL	LAST
				GI	11.30	11.60	GMJUL45	.10	.20	SI				
				GJ	6.80	7.00	GMJUL50	.45	.60	SJ				
3.20	3.30	3.05	120	GK	3.20	3.30	GMJUL55	1.75	1.85	SK	1.85	1.80	73	1.85
1.10	1.25	1.05	266	GL	1.10	1.20	GMJUL60	4.60	4.80	SL	4.70	4.70	20	4.70
.40	.50	.35	64	GM	.40	.45	GMJUL65	9.20	9.40	SM				

Table and prices provided by PreferredTrade, Inc.

Since you believe GM will move above $60 per share with no problem, your first inclination is to buy the July 60 call, priced at $1.20 (or $120 for the full contract). But, on further thought, you realize that GM would have to climb nearly $4 a share just to keep you from suffering a total loss. You wouldn't break even until the stock got to $61.20 — and GM would have to hit $62.40 before you'd double your money (and that doesn't even allow for commissions). You're bullish — but not quite that bullish. So, you look at the July 55 call.

The ask price for that option is $3.30, or $330 total, and the prospects for success look a bit more positive. GM would have to fall $1.10 a share before you'd suffer a total loss, and you'd need a move of only $2.20 a share—to $58.30—to break even. But, you'd still need a move to $61.60 to double your money. Certainly not impossible—but not exactly guaranteed either. So, what do you do?

In this situation, the optimum alternative is a vertical bull spread. If you buy the GM July 55 call at $3.30 ($330) and simultaneously sell the July 60 call at $1.10 ($110), your net cost is $2.20 ($220)—which is also your maximum risk. Plus, you get a highly positive scenario. GM's stock needs to rise just $1.10, to $57.20, for you to break even, and a move of only $3.30, to $59.40, will double your money. Tack on just 60 cents more and you get the maximum profit for the position of $2.80, or $280—which represents a seven-week return of 109 percent, even after commissions of around $40. (Most brokers count a spread order as one order, with only one commission.) Quite a satisfactory potential outcome—especially since we already know you feel fairly sure GM's headed for the $60-plus level.

Given that, you call up the "Spread" panel on your broker's order-entry screen, plug in the specifics of the trade you want to open—as shown in the sample screen in Figure 2-4 on page 46—and press the "Send" button. (You can either specify the exchange where you want the order sent or let the program automatically route it to the exchange with the best price.) And, as with a single-option order, because you're trading under 20 contracts at the market price, the orders will be filled automatically in a matter of seconds, with the confirmations coming back to the "Filled Orders" section of your screen. (*Note: As trading technology improves and the ECNs grow more sophisticated, it may soon be possible for the two sides of a spread to be filled on differing exchanges, with the computer automatically routing the buy order to the site with the lowest ask and the sell order to the one with the highest bid, thus holding the total cost to its absolute minimum. For now, however, both spread fills will come from the same exchange unless you choose to manually leg in or out.*)

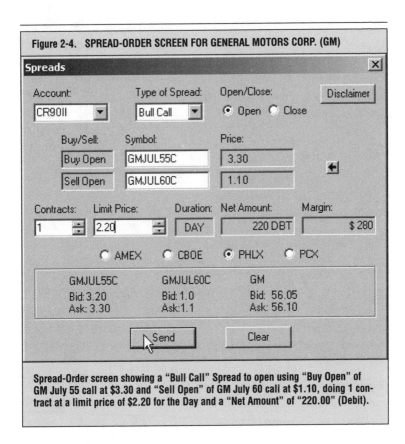

Figure 2-4. SPREAD-ORDER SCREEN FOR GENERAL MOTORS CORP. (GM)

Spread-Order screen showing a "Bull Call" Spread to open using "Buy Open" of GM July 55 call at $3.30 and "Sell Open" of GM July 60 call at $1.10, doing 1 contract at a limit price of $2.20 for the Day and a "Net Amount" of "220.00" (Debit).

Once the expiration date rolls around—or earlier if you achieve a nice profit and want to grab it—you have several alternatives for exiting. If GM's stock has fallen below $55 a share, you simply let both calls expire, taking the maximum loss. If GM is above $55, but below $60, you sell the long 55 call and let the short 60 call expire, taking either a partial profit or partial loss, depending on the exact stock price. And, if GM moves above $60 as expected—either before or at expiration—you sell the July 55 call and buy back the July 60, earning the spread's maximum profit (less any bid/ask differential).

You can do this on the "Spread" order screen by simply reversing your previous instructions—i.e., changing the July 55 order from

"Buy Open" to "Sell Close" and the July 60 from "Sell Open" to "Buy Close"—and then submitting it as a single order. Or, you can "leg out"—closing each side in a separate transaction. Having these two alternatives provides an advantage in your online trading as it greatly increases your flexibility in determining an exit strategy and thereby boosting your profit potential. For example, you can choose the former course when both options have moved fairly deep in the money, or when they're nearing expiration, and you want to ensure a risk-free exit. By contrast, the latter would be your choice should the underlying stock make a sharp early move that shows signs of continuing, prompting a desire to buy back your short option and hold the long option to pursue speculative profits in excess of the spread's original maximum.

If that sounds like a lot of possibilities, it is—but this merely illustrates the versatility of both options in general and vertical spreads in particular. And we haven't even considered some of the alternatives for changing the aggressiveness of your speculation using vertical spreads. These include:

- Positioning a deep in-the-money spread—say, a July 50/55 call spread when the stock price is at $56 or $57 a share. This is considered a conservative play, in that it has a high probability of success (the stock can actually fall in price and you'll still make the maximum profit), but the potential profit is fairly small relative to the possible loss. (In the GM situation just discussed, the 50/55 call spread had a cost/risk of $3.80 versus a maximum potential profit of just $1.20, but would have generated that gain even if the stock had fallen $1.20 to $55 per share.)

- Positioning an out-of-the-money spread—perhaps a July 60/65 spread when the stock is at $57 or $58. This is considered extremely aggressive, in that it has a very low probability of success. However, it has a low cost and produces a large percentage profit when it does work. (In the GM example, the 60/65 call spread cost just 80 cents and had a maximum potential profit of $4.20, but required the stock to climb $8.80 a share—to $65— to generate that profit.)

- Positioning a spread with a wider strike-price range—perhaps $7.50 or $10.00. This also tends to be considered more aggressive. It has a higher cost and risk, but also a larger potential real-dollar profit. As such, short-term traders tend to reserve the wider spreads for volatile stocks or market indexes, while longer-term investors favor them for more stable stocks that tend to move in trends.

Why Opt for Vertical Credit Spreads?

The latter of those alternatives, the wider strike-price range, is also popular among traders who like to employ the other two kinds of vertical spreads—i.e., those that produce a credit when opened. With a wider strike-price spread, more cash is brought into their accounts up front—and, while the credit (and, perhaps, a margin deposit) must stay there for the duration of the trade—it's still better than having to pay out premium debits to open a position. Using puts for bullish trades and calls for bearish ones may also produce more favorable risk/reward ratios than debit spreads with the same strike prices. In addition, if the spread works perfectly, both options expire worthless and you save the closing commissions. The following tables detail the specifics of the vertical credit spreads.

Strategy 7—A Bullish Vertical Put Spread

Trade Description: Buy a put option, typically at or just out of the money, and simultaneously sell another put option on the same stock and with the same expiration date, but with a *higher* strike price.

Expectation: The price of the underlying stock will *rise* above the strike price of the put sold by the expiration date, thereby rendering both puts worthless and allowing you to keep the credit received at the time the spread was initiated.

Break-Even Point: The strike price of the put sold, minus the per-share credit received when the trade was opened.

Potential Profit: Limited to the credit received at the time the trade was initiated.

Maximum Risk: Limited to the difference between the two strike prices, less the opening credit received (the per-share credit x 100 x number of contracts).

Cost to Open: Commission only, but credit received must stay in account.

Margin Requirement: Exchange minimum (the maximum amount at risk), or greater at your broker's discretion.

Strategy 8—A Bearish Vertical Call Spread

Trade Description: Buy a call option, typically at or just out of the money, and simultaneously sell another call option on the same underlying stock and with the same expiration date, but with a *lower* strike price.

Expectation: The price of the stock will *fall* below the strike price of the call sold by the expiration date, at which time both calls will then expire worthless, allowing you to keep the credit received when the spread was positioned.

Break-Even Point: The strike price of the call sold, plus the credit received when the trade was opened.

Potential Profit: Limited to the credit received when the trade was initiated.

Maximum Risk: Limited to the difference between the two strike prices, less the opening credit received (the per-share credit x 100 x number of contracts).

Cost to Open: Commission only, but credit received must stay in account.

Margin Requirement: Exchange minimum, or greater at broker's discretion.

A Quick Look at Other Combination Strategies

There are several types of spreads other than vertical ones—including calendar (or time) spreads, which involve buying and selling options with different expiration dates, and so-called butterfly spreads, which feature two long and two short calls with three different strike prices. There are also a variety of other combination strategies that utilize two or more differing options to create low-risk or high-profit scenarios suitable for either ultra-stable or highly volatile market situations.

Thorough discussion of these strategies must rightly be reserved for more comprehensive books on options trading—especially since the software currently provided by the majority of today's online brokerage firms still doesn't allow for direct entry of most combination orders. That doesn't, of course, mean you can't do such strategies online. You merely have to use a little extra thought —and a little added caution—in placing your opening and closing orders.

The order-entry software I use at PreferredTrade includes a "staging" feature—also offered by many other brokers—that is ideal for this purpose. It allows you to enter the specifics for each individual option you wish to buy or sell as part of a combination strategy, and put them on hold until you have all the orders for a given trade ready to send. You can then release them in rapid succession so that all legs of your combination, regardless of how complex, are filled within seconds of one another.

One warning, however: The loss limits in virtually every combination strategy apply **only** if you get fills on **both** the long and short options. In other words, you do not want to wind up **just short a call or put**, without owning the corresponding option that covers it.

The best way to avoid such a problem when initiating your online strategies is to stage all the orders, then send the buy orders first— releasing the sell orders only when you receive a confirmation back on your "Filled Orders" screen. That way, should something happen and your "Sell Open" order not go through to complete the combination, your risk on the unintended one-sided position will be limited to the amount you paid for the option(s) you bought. You also won't face a hefty margin requirement. Absent those pressures, you'll have time to either re-evaluate your desire to do the trade—or adjust the specified price on the short option and try your sale order again.

It Works With Covered Calls, Too

That approach can also be used when you're placing orders for strategies involving both options and stocks, such as the final one we want to discuss in this Key Step—and the only option technique permitted by most brokers in Individual Retirement Accounts (IRAs). This strategy is known as covered call writing.

Historically, covered call writing has been used almost exclusively by stock owners as a strategy to increase the flow of income from their holdings, over and above what they collect in dividends. Typically, a stock owner will sell an out-of-the-money call option with enough life remaining to make the premium worth collecting. The optimum result would then be to have the option expire worthless, which would allow the seller to keep both the stock and the full premium received for selling the call. If that happens, the strategy can be repeated with the same stock, but using calls from a new option cycle.

Alternately, if the stock price climbs to a level above the call's strike price, the shares will be called away at the option's expiration. That produces a profit on the stock, and the seller again gets to keep the premium received for the call. However, commissions—sometimes quite high—are incurred on the sale of the stock, future dividends are lost and the owner is left with a hole in his portfolio and excess cash that needs to be put to work. As a result, stock owners in this situation often choose to buy back the short calls rather than letting the shares be called away. While that reduces the profit and return on the play, it's still better than the worst possible result. That occurs when the stock falls in price by an amount greater than the premium received for the call, thereby producing a loss on the overall strategy.

Whether it works perfectly or not, covered call writing remains a popular strategy among both conventional and online traders. However, generation of added income is no longer the sole objective of those using the technique. Indeed, the combination of higher option premiums (a result of increased market volatility in recent years), guaranteed executions on electronic trades and sharply lower commissions has greatly increased the use of covered call writing as a short-term speculative strategy.

Traders who think a stock may be ready to make a modest up-move—often by as little as a couple of dollars—will purchase the shares and write nearby out-of-the-money calls, using the premium received to reduce their cost basis. The option sale may be done simultaneously or, if the trader is more aggressive, it may be delayed a few days to allow the stock price to rise, resulting in a higher premium. Either way, the trader's hope is that the stock price will rise above the option strike price at expiration, the calls will be exercised and the shares called away. If that happens, the trader will net a profit equal to the difference between the stock's purchase price and the call strike price, plus the premium received, less commissions. On stocks in the $20 to $40 price range, this can frequently return 10 to 15 percent in a month to six weeks — which makes for a quite generous annualized payback.

Whatever your goal in initiating a covered call writing strategy, you'll find it's both easier and safer to place your orders online than through a conventional broker. You simply call up the online broker's order-entry screen, click on the "Stock" button in the "Order Type" box, fill in the particulars regarding the underlying stock on which you want to write covered calls and hit the "Stage" button. You then switch to "Option" in the "Order Type" box, designate the order as a "Sell Open," fill in the option specifics, including price, and "Stage" that order as well. Once both orders are staged, you release the stock order and wait — usually only a matter of seconds — until you receive a confirmation on your "Filled Orders" screen, at which point you release the option order, which should fill automatically if you've priced it at the market. Figure 2-5 on the opposite page shows how your order-entry screen might look in the middle of initiating a covered call writing strategy on Dell Computer.

By entering your orders in this fashion, you guarantee that you'll always own the underlying stock *before* your short option position is created, thus eliminating any worries about a large margin requirement or the potential for unlimited option risk that would result from being short "naked" calls.

By staging the orders and having them filled in sequence, you also gain the flexibility to seek better prices for both the stock and the option if you want. In other words, if you buy the stock and simultaneously sell the calls, it's almost mandatory that you use a market order for the stock, simply because you can't afford the risk of selling the options and not getting the covering stock. However, when you stage your orders, you can set a limit price on the stock, release the order and let it work until it's filled. Once that happens

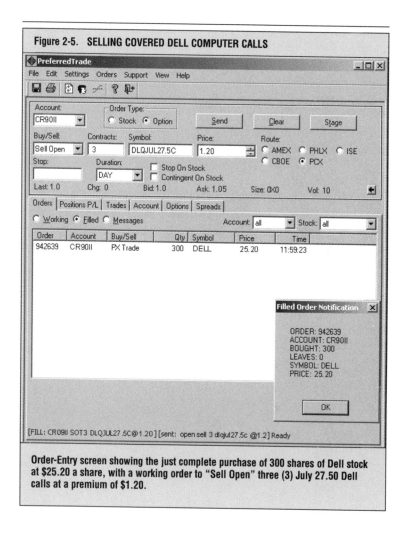

Figure 2-5. SELLING COVERED DELL COMPUTER CALLS

Order-Entry screen showing the just complete purchase of 300 shares of Dell stock at $25.20 a share, with a working order to "Sell Open" three (3) July 27.50 Dell calls at a premium of $1.20.

and you know you're covered, you can then release a limit order for the calls and let it work for several hours—or even several days—until you get the premium you want.

This can add several percentage points to your return on a short-term covered call play—though some investors with a "set-it-and-forget-it" mindset might feel it is more trouble than it's worth. The important thing, however, is that you have the option. By trading online, you can do it your way—and you don't have to make a phone call or bother a human broker every 30 minutes to make your trades happen.

A Final Word on Strategies

As we've already noted, there are probably at least two dozen additional option strategies you can use—and several books' worth of details you can study about analyzing option values and identifying the best trading opportunities. Providing such comprehensive information is beyond both the scope and the intent of this book. What we have tried to do in this Key Step is give you a glimpse at the many possible option-trading strategies, as well as illustrating that, whichever technique you choose to use, there is a way to do it online.

And, in most cases, it's probably an easier, faster and cheaper way to boot!

Chapter 3

KEY STEP NO. 3:
Choose the Proper Underlying Assets

A lthough they are traded as separate and unique securities, the essence of every option lies in *its underlying asset*— be it 100 shares of common stock, a leading market index, a foreign currency or any other item of value.

The importance of this seemingly simple fact cannot be overstated if you hope to be successful as an options trader—either online or off. That's because the characteristics of the underlying security will determine both the *premium you pay* (or receive) for the options you trade and your chances for success with *the strategies you choose* to use them in.

For example, assume you've been following a stock that has traded in a range of, say, $20 to $24 per share over the past six months. Obviously, options on that stock would be very poor candidates for a strategy requiring either a $5-per-share price move or a rise above $25 to produce positive results. If you wanted to sell options on that stock, it would also be unlikely you'd get premiums high enough to make many strategies worthwhile. (See the box on the pages 56 and 57 for a review of how option premiums are determined.)

Likewise, if you were interested in doing a stable-market option strategy—say, a butterfly spread or a short straddle—your odds of success would literally plummet if you tried it on a volatile market index or a stock that had traded in a range from $25 to $55 during the past six months.

Key Elements of an Option Premium

The price a buyer pays when he purchases an option—or receives when he sells one—is known as the premium. The buyer must pay the full premium at the time of the purchase (option premiums are *not* marginable), and the seller gets to keep it regardless of whether the option is subsequently exercised or not. Premiums are quoted on a per-share basis. Thus, a quoted premium of $1.25 represents an actual payment of $125 on a standard 100-share stock option contract.

The actual size of the premium for any given option is determined by a number of factors, the three most important being:

- The strike price of the option relative to the actual price of the underlying asset, which is known as the intrinsic value.
- The length of time remaining prior to the option's expiration date, called the time value.
- The degree to which the price of the underlying asset fluctuates, referred to as the volatility value.

A basic formula for option pricing could thus be:

Intrinsic Value + Time Value + Volatility Value = Option Premium

Unfortunately, the only absolute in that equation is the intrinsic value. To illustrate, assume XYZ stock was trading at $33 per share and you purchased an October XYZ call with a $30 strike price, paying a premium of $5.50 per share. The intrinsic value of the call would be $3.00 a share—always the difference between the actual stock price and the call's strike price. (By contrast, a $35 call would have no intrinsic value because its strike price would be above the actual stock price, while a $35 put would have an intrinsic value of $2.00 per share—again, the difference between the strike price and the actual stock price.)

The remaining $2.50 of the $5.50 call premium would be attributed to a combination of time value and volatility value. While there's no simple way to determine an exact breakdown (there are complicated mathematical formulas, typically using the Black-Scholes option-pricing model or variations thereof), two basics apply:

1. The more time remaining until the option's expiration, the greater the time value portion of the premium.
2. The greater the volatility of the underlying asset, the higher the volatility portion of the premium.

Thus, in our October XYZ example, time value would likely dominate the non-intrinsic portion of the premium in August, while volatility value would be a greater consideration in early October, after most of the time value had eroded.

A number of other elements also play minor roles in determining a fair premium for an option, factoring into either the time value or volatility value. These are:

- The quality of the underlying stock.
- The dividend rate of the underlying stock.
- The present level of interest rates.
- Prevailing market conditions.
- Supply and demand for options involving the underlying stock.

Continued on next Page

So, how do you go about choosing the proper underlying assets for the option strategies you want to employ? There are a number of tools to help you, starting with the charting service featured in the software packages or websites of most leading online brokerage firms. For example, on the PreferredTrade website, two clicks of the mouse and entry of a stock symbol will retrieve a basic chart, provided by Quote.com, similar to the one shown in Figure 3-1 on page 58. Even if you have no experience at all in technical analysis or determining volatility ratings, a quick glance at a basic chart like this will tell you whether the stock you're considering has been trading tamely or taking investors on a wild ride. You can also gauge its position relative to its moving average and note any changes in its trading volume—two indicators that frequently point to an impending price move.

Using "Beta" As a Strategic Tool

A second means of determining which stocks might work best with which option strategies is to review the "beta coefficient" of the stocks you're considering. "Beta" is simply a Greek letter designating the measure of a stock's volatility relative to the market as a whole. If a stock has a beta of 1.00, it means it will generally move in precise step with the overall market. A beta greater than 1.00 means the stock's price movements will be more volatile than those of the total market, while a beta less than 1.00 means the share price will be less volatile than the market.

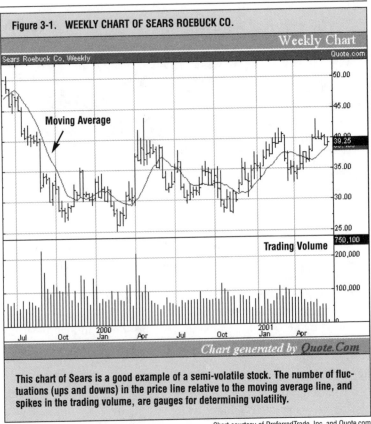

Figure 3-1. WEEKLY CHART OF SEARS ROEBUCK CO.

Weekly Chart
Quote.com

Sears Roebuck Co, Weekly

Moving Average

Trading Volume

This chart of Sears is a good example of a semi-volatile stock. The number of fluctuations (ups and downs) in the price line relative to the moving average line, and spikes in the trading volume, are gauges for determining volatility.

Chart courtesy of PreferredTrade, Inc. and Quote.com

Given that, a fairly standard approach would be to use options on stocks with a high beta for strategies that require large relative moves for success, and options on stocks with low betas for stable-market strategies. Examples of the former might be long straddles or outright speculations involving call or put purchases, while samples of the latter might include a five-point vertical bull or bear spread or a covered call write on a stock being held primarily for income, rather than appreciation.

The websites of many online brokerages—or those of other free Internet market sites, such as CBS MarketWatch.com® or CNBC.com® —provide snapshots of basic fundamental data, including the beta, on most optionable stocks, so the information is fairly easy to find. In addition, though it's not absolutely necessary, if you're really serious about becoming a successful options trader, you'll probably want to take advantage of one of the special integrated trading offers available through most online brokers. These deals will give you special client rates on proprietary software packages (some of which run well into the four-figure range), as well as access to the data bases and quote systems of such popular analytical services as OptionVue Systems, eSignal, QCharts, DTNIQ, Equis, AT Financial and others.

Integrated Trading — A Valuable Extra

Depending on their specialty, these services will provide all the fundamental and technical information you could possibly need about the stocks you're working with, as well as detailed charts for various time periods, option valuations and a host of other information. Perhaps most valuable, however, is the screening process the leading software packages will perform for you. All you have to do is specify the type of strategy you want to do, the risk/reward parameters you're looking for and any other key trading criteria you want to impose. The computer program will then run through all stocks and corresponding options, looking for combinations that fulfill your criteria, and signal you when it finds one or more. You can then review the details, decide if the potential trade's to your liking and place your order. Typically, the analytical pages of these services will interact directly with your online broker's order-entry software so you don't even have to switch back and forth from screen to screen. You can enter an order right where you are — and immediately resume looking for the next promising opportunity.

Many of these integrated services — as well as the better online brokerage programs — will also monitor all of your open positions, updating prices and values as the market changes. If you've specified profit targets, stop-losses or other exit points, the programs will signal you when they're reached — or, depending on the program and your desires, automatically close out the trades.

All in all, the combination of direct access to current market news, quotes and charts; online stock analysis; and computerized option valuation and screening has made it far easier to structure potentially lucrative options strategies—and to ensure that you're using them with the underlying assets most likely to produce success.

Using Your Tools to Pick a Stock

So you can see just how helpful the computerized monitoring functions can be in selecting stocks for your online options-trading program, and in actually executing trades, we'll look at a couple of examples. For starters, let's assume it's mid-April and you think the market may enjoy a modest rally over the coming month. You'd like to grab some short-term profits from the expected move, but you don't want to simply buy calls and take the risk of an outright speculation. You're not averse to purchasing shares in a high-beta stock that might outpace the market in an upmove, but you'd also like to give yourself a little extra edge. So, you decide to try a short-term covered write.

Not wanting to tie up more than about $7,500 on the play, you decide you'll look for stocks under $25, buy 300 shares and write three out-of-the-money May calls. Just for the sake of contrasts, let's say you had already noticed a pair of stocks in that price range, so you decide to give them a look. The first is Kroger Co., the big grocery chain, trading at about $23.50, and the second is Advanced Micro Devices (AMD), the computer chip manufacturer, trading at around $24.50.

Your initial step in deciding between the two is to check a chart of each stock, which you can request from your broker's website. With only a cursory glance, you can see that AMD looks more promising since it has been trading in a range between $20 and $30 for most of the year and is currently trending higher from its most recent low. Kroger, on the other hand, has been trading between $22.50 and $25.50 and is moving down from the top of that range. A quick check of the betas for both stocks tips the scales further toward AMD. Its beta is 2.27, which means it will likely advance more strongly than the market on any rally, whereas Kroger's beta is a minuscule 0.05, meaning it will probably lag the market substantially on a coming upmove.

Finally, you check the actual option prices and find that the Kroger May 25 call, the nearest out-of-the-money call, is bid at only 70 cents, a reflection of the stock's ultra-low beta. Obviously, a premium that low makes Kroger a poor choice speculative covered write, since the maximum profit, should the stock actually move above $25, would be just $2.20 ($1.50 on the stock's rise to $25, plus 70 cents for the options)—or $660 total on a three-call position. Subtract commissions of about $50 ($15 each way on the stock and $20 on the options) and you get a net of $610, which would represent a return of 8.65 percent on the initial outlay of $7,050. That's not bad for a one-month play, but it's based on the assumption everything works perfectly—which is unlikely, given Kroger's low beta, recent trading range and current trend. It also pales compared to the AMD alternative.

That's because the AMD May 25 call is priced at $3.40, quite rich for an option still 50 cents out of the money, and the May 27.5 call is bid at $2.05. These large premiums, of course, reflect AMD's high volatility, as denoted by its 2.27 beta. Discarding the May 25 call because it doesn't allow room for the stock to move, you check the numbers for the May 27.5 call and discover an extremely attractive scenario. If AMD moves above $27.50 at expiration, you'll gain $3.00 on the stock, plus the $2.05 received for the calls—or $5.50 total. That's $550 per contract, or $1,650 for the full three-contract position. Subtract $50 in commissions and you net $1,600—a return of 21.76 percent on the initial investment of $7,350. That's an outstanding potential outcome—and the odds of achieving it are also high, given AMD's trading range, trend and volatility rating.

In fact, that result actually was achieved in this case. All of the numbers cited in the above example were real, and AMD not only topped $27.50 by the May expiration, but climbed all the way to $34. Kroger also fulfilled its expectations, rallying slightly with the market, but settling back to close at just $24 a share when the May options expired.

Taking Advantage of Conditional Orders

Before you become concerned that the analytical process just described seems overly complicated, especially for just two stocks, rest assured that we've taken what is essentially a simple procedure and made it complex, solely for purposes of illustration. In the real-life world of online options trading, you won't have to go through nearly that much hassle. Instead, you'll merely enter the parameters of the stocks and options you're seeking for a particular strategy, then let a computer-screening program do the analytical work for you. It will automatically eliminate all the poor choices (like Kroger and its options), and present only the best opportunities for your consideration (like the AMD combination).

In addition, once an opportunity is identified, you won't be compelled to act on it immediately. Rather, you'll be able to utilize one of the many features of your online broker's software program to monitor the stocks and options under consideration, and enter your order only if prospects for success actually improve. This process is referred to as using "conditional orders," and it's available with most state-of-the-art online brokerage programs.

There are two types of conditional option orders. The first is referred to as a "contingent-on-stock" order, while the second is called a "stop-on-stock" order. These orders, which are essentially the opposite of one another, enable you to either open or close an option position when the underlying stock (or market index) trades at specified price above or below its current level. To be precise:

- An *opening* contingent-on-stock order can be used to *buy a call* or *sell a put short* should the price of the underlying stock (or index) *move down* from its present level.

- An *opening* contingent-on-stock order can be used to *sell a call short* or *buy a put* should the price of the underlying stock (or index) *move up* from its present level.

- A *closing* contingent-on-stock order can be used to *sell a long call* or *cover a short put* should the price of the underlying stock (or index) *move up* from its present level.

- A *closing* contingent-on-stock order can be used to *cover a short call* or *sell a long put* should the price of the underlying stock (or index) *move down* from its present level.

- An *opening* stop-on-stock order can be used to *buy a call* or *sell a put short* should the price of the underlying stock (or index) *move up* from its present level.

- An *opening* stop-on-stock order can be used to *sell a call short* or *buy a put* should the price of the underlying stock (or index) *move down* from its present level.

- A *closing* stop-on-stock order can be used to *sell a long call* or *cover a short put* should the price of the underlying stock (or index) *move down* from its present level.

- A *closing* stop-on-stock order can be used to *cover a short call* or *sell a long put* should the price of the underlying stock (or index) *move up* from its present level.

With conditional orders—whether contingent-on-stock or stop-on-stock—you have a wide range of strategic alternatives. For example, you can buy a stock when you think it's at a bargain price level, then put in a good-till-canceled (GTC) contingent order to write covered calls against it—but *only* if the price of the stock rises to a specified level. This will generally earn you a larger premium on the sale of the call, thereby lowering your cost basis on the stock and sharply increasing your potential return on the entire position. Or, you can buy an in-the-money put option on a stock that you think is going to decline in price, then place a GTC stop order to sell a lower-strike-price put, thereby creating a vertical bear spread—but *only* if the price of the underlying stock falls to a specified level. This will generally result in a far narrower spread—meaning you'll have a much lower maximum risk (or, occasionally, no risk at all) and a much larger maximum profit.

Contingent orders can also be used to trigger the initial purchase of a call should the underlying stock fall to a support level, or to spur the opening purchase of a put should the underlying stock climb to a resistance point. In similar fashion, stop-on-stock orders can initiate the short sale of a put should the underlying stock break through a moving average or resistance level, or spark the short

Why Not 'Contingent-on-Option-Price' Orders?

Most brokers don't permit "contingent" orders based on option prices—as opposed to stock prices—and most traders wouldn't be comfortable using them if they did. Why? The basic reason is that changes in option premiums are far from predictable—even when the price of the underlying stock moves as expected. As already explained, there are three primary components to an option premium—intrinsic value (I), time value (T) and volatility value (V). However, the relationship among the three changes constantly, and often by greatly varying degrees. For example, the I-T-V value relationship on an out-of-the-money call with three weeks of life left might be 0%-70%-30%. But, a week later, after the underlying stock has risen by, say, $4 per share, it could be 25%-35%-40%. And, another week later, after another $4 rise in the stock price, it could be 65%-10%-25%. Finally, after one more week with no change in the stock price, it would be 100%-0%-0%.

This explains why many people find analyzing the possible outcome of option strategies so difficult. They can't estimate the inherent time and volatility value in an option premium, so they can't accurately project possible future results—unless they assume the options will be held until expiration. At that point, they will no longer have any time or volatility value, so an accurate assessment of the trade results can be made. In practice, however, most options are not held until they expire, but are sold (or bought back) prior to expiration—when both time and volatility still play a role, albeit a variable one, in determining the size of the option premium. Thus, when placing conditional orders, it's only sensible to base them on the more predictable stock price, rather than guessing what level the actual option premium might reach.

---

sale of a call if the stock falls through a support level. Both types of orders can also be used to take profits on winning positions when target prices are reached, or to protect profits by closing out when prices reverse.

Conditional orders are also extremely popular with day traders, who use them with both index options and options on highly volatile individual stocks. The actual strategies vary, depending on the market climate and the orientation of the trader. However, a common play involves initiating long option positions if such widely followed indexes as the S&P 500 or Nasdaq Composite open up (or down) by a certain amount, then setting conditional exit targets based on expected later-day moves by the underlying index. Many day traders also place conditional stop orders to buy calls if an upward trending stock opens higher (or puts, if a downward trending stock opens lower). If the contingency is met, the expectation is that the stock will continue to advance (or decline) by a sufficient amount over the course of the day to produce a worthwhile profit on the option, which will typically be cashed in shortly before the close.

Entering Your Conditional Orders

Whatever strategy you use contingent or stop-on-stock orders for — whether long term or in day trading — you'll have no trouble placing them with most of today's online brokerage software packages. To illustrate, consider the following example:

Assume you own 400 shares of Sears stock, which you bought several months ago at $34 per share. You feel the retail sector will do well as the economy improves, so you're hoping for some long-term capital appreciation. In the meantime, you're collecting the 92-cent-a-share dividend — $368 a year on your 400 shares, or a fairly paltry 2.7 percent yield on your initial cost of $13,600. You'd like to augment that by writing some covered calls, but the only ones worth selling are the July 35s — and you don't want to risk having the stock called away at that price. However, the stock's showing signs of entering an uptrend, so you decide to watch it for a few days. Sure enough, it gradually eases higher until, a little over a week later, it breaks through its 50-day moving average and shoots up to $38 a share.

Willing to risk having the stock called away at $40 a share, you decide to write the July 40 calls — but *only* if the stock continues to advance and hits $39.50, which should boost the premium to around $1.60 per share. If that happens, and the stock is still above $40 when the July calls expire in six weeks, your profit will be $6.00 per share on the stock, plus $1.60 on the calls, or $7.60 total. That would equate to $3,040 on the full position, less commissions (which would be more than covered by the quarterly dividend you received) — giving you a 22.35 percent return in under six months. And, if the contingent order is tripped, but the stock slips back

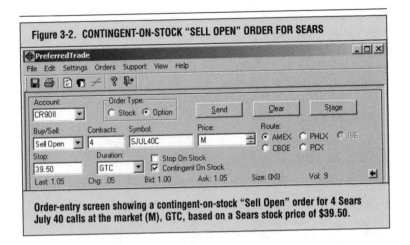

Figure 3-2. CONTINGENT-ON-STOCK "SELL OPEN" ORDER FOR SEARS

Order-entry screen showing a contingent-on-stock "Sell Open" order for 4 Sears July 40 calls at the market (M), GTC, based on a Sears stock price of $39.50.

below $40 by the July expiration, you simply keep the $1.60 ($640) premium received, viewing it either as added income or as reducing your original cost basis in the stock to $32.40 a share.

Happy with either of those potential outcomes, you go ahead and place a contingent-on-stock order to sell four July 40 Sears calls at the market, contingent on Sears stock rising in price to $39.50 a share. Figure 3-2 shows how the transaction would look on your broker's order-entry screen.

A Day Trading Example — With Conditions

Just to ensure you're clear on the process, we'll look at one more example — this time using a stop-on-stock order for a short-term play. Assume it's early June and you've been following the recent gyrations of Texas Instruments, which has been posting day-to-day price moves of $2.50 to $3.50 per share as it trades up and down between $32 and $42 a share. In the past four sessions, the stock fell $10 a share, bottoming at $32.25 before bouncing to close yesterday at $34.75. The overall market also closed strong and indications are it could continue higher in today's session, most likely carrying TXN with it.

You'd like to take a shot at a day trade, but you don't want to lay out the cash required to purchase the stock—or take the high-dollar risk such a play would entail should TXN drop. You also don't want to lay out the high premiums the recent volatility has generated in the July Texas Instruments calls. However, the June 35 calls, with just four days of life left, show promise. The current ask price is 70 cents, or $70 per contract, which you're willing to risk—but *only* if TXN stock opens higher, hitting at least $35.00. If that happens, the price on the June 35 calls would probably jump to 80 cents, but that would still be a bargain—if TXN stock gains $2.50 on the day, as it did the prior session. That would carry the stock to around $37.25 near the close—meaning the June 35 call should have a premium of around $2.60 ($2.25 intrinsic value, plus a time/volatility value of 35 cents or so). Closing out before the final bell would thus net a profit of around $1.80—or $1,800 on a 10-option position (less $40 in commissions).

That's quite a potential coup on a day trade with a maximum risk estimated at only $800, so you decide to give it a go. You call up your broker's order-entry screen and type in the data needed to "Buy Open" 10 June 35 Texas Instruments calls at the market, contingent on a stop price of $35 on the stock. The exact appearance of the screen is shown in Figure 3-3 below.

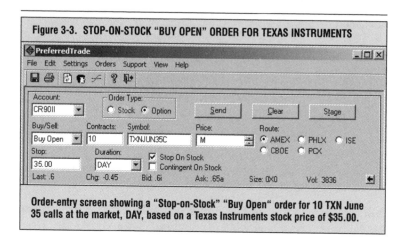

Figure 3-3. STOP-ON-STOCK "BUY OPEN" ORDER FOR TEXAS INSTRUMENTS

Order-entry screen showing a "Stop-on-Stock" "Buy Open" order for 10 TXN June 35 calls at the market, DAY, based on a Texas Instruments stock price of $35.00.

A Final Word on Conditional Orders

Obviously, conditional orders won't be suitable for most of the strategies you may want to employ—or for every underlying asset on which you trade options. Where they can be used, though, they can give you a significant advantage in tailoring your trades and getting the prices you want. However, you must be careful to properly enter your orders. While it's likely your broker's software will invalidate any erroneous entries—or market conditions will make them impossible to fill—getting them right is still your responsibility when trading online. You don't have a live broker to back you up, so it's best to pay close attention to what you're doing and not make any mistakes in the first place.

Always remember, too, that your primary focus should still be on the actual option premium you want to pay (or receive)—even when using conditional orders. Ask yourself what circumstances will cause the price of the option to go up, and what will cause it to go down. Then set your contingent or stop price accordingly. For example, if you want to protect a put position you own with a stop-on-stock order, your stop price would be *above the current stock price* since this would translate to *a lower put price*. Thus, your stop order—though contingent on a rising stock price—would actually be an order to sell *below* the current market price for the put. The following should clarify the pricing objectives you should have when using the two different types of conditional orders:

- Contingent-on-stock *BUY* orders—for either calls or puts—are used when you want a price *BELOW* the current market price of the option.

- Contingent-on-stock *SELL* orders are used when you want a price *ABOVE* the current market price of the option.

- Stop-on-stock *BUY* orders—for either calls or puts—are used when you want a price *ABOVE* the current market price of the option.

- Stop-on-stock *SELL* orders—for either calls or puts—are used when you want a price *BELOW* the current market price of the option.

Also be aware that, while you *may* specify a limit price for the option you're buying or selling with a conditional order, your odds of getting a successful execution of the trade are far, far higher if you simply enter "m" in the option "Price" field—meaning you'll accept a fill at whatever the market price of the option is when the stock price eventually triggers the trade. As noted in the box featured a couple of pages ago, the time and volatility variables make estimating what an option premium might be at some future time an extremely difficult endeavor. Thus, if you insist on specifying a limit on the option price as well as a contingent stock price, chances are you may never get the exact conditions needed for a fill.

With those final admonitions about choosing the best underlying assets and placing the proper orders to open your option positions, let's now take a look at some of the best strategies for getting out of them.

Chapter 4

KEY STEP NO. 4:
Plan an Appropriate Exit Strategy

We won't pretend to be able to tell you when you should get out of any option position—whether it's an outright speculation involving a long call or put, a relatively conservative play such as a covered call write, or a day trade using highly volatile index options. Only *you* can decide how much risk you want to take and how large a profit you want to aim for—a decision you'll no doubt base on your well-thought-out investment objectives, exaggerated by your innate sense of greed, then tempered by your inability to sleep at night in the face of ever-present market uncertainties.

What we will do is offer one basic piece of advice—essential for anyone who hopes to succeed as an active options trader:

> Any time you open a new position involving options
> —regardless of the strategy you're using—
> **immediately plan an appropriate exit strategy.**

That means setting *both a specific loss limit and an expected profit target* for every trade you do. It also means designating those benchmarks based on solid reasoning and sound market logic, not raw emotion—as well as developing the personal fortitude to stay within the boundaries you set. If you feel such stringent guidelines are too restrictive for your tastes, and start looking for ways to work around them, then you are almost certainly headed for eventual trading disappointment—if not outright disaster. Especially if it's the loss side of the equation on which you're trying to hedge.

Indeed, while most profit targets should have some "wiggle room" to allow for the pursuit of added gains (we'll discuss ways to get such flexibility in a few minutes), *your loss limits should be absolute!*

The Art of Setting Loss Limits

In other words, once you decide the maximum risk exposure you want to accept, *stick with it* — no matter what may happen with the specific underlying asset or the market in general. However, the fact that your loss limit is absolute doesn't mean it should be arbitrary — nor does it mean it should be the same for every strategy.

In some instances, say with the speculative purchase of an out-of-the-money call or put, the play itself may define the risk limit — i.e., your decision to pay the premium of 70 or 80 cents expresses your willingness to lose the entire amount on what's essentially a long-shot bet. However, the mere fact that a given strategy has a maximum risk doesn't mean you have to accept the loss of the entire amount. For example, if you buy an in-the-money call for $8.00 or $9.00, expecting an upmove, you might plan to close out and take a partial loss should the stock price, instead, fall back to the option's strike-price level. Or, if you are a market technician, you might opt to key your call (or put) loss limits to a stock's support (or resistance) level, closing if it's penetrated.

Vertical bull or bear spreads, which can result in a total loss on a fairly small price move if held to expiration, may also be candidates for an early exit. For example, you may plan to close on any countermove by the stock to a level beyond the strike price of your long option, choosing to take a modest loss and look for new opportunities, rather than hoping for a rebound and possibly losing it all. Or, you may plan to use any early pullback as an opportunity to leg out of the spread, actually upping your maximum loss — but also opening the way to unlimited profits should the underlying stock or index rebound.

With many strategies involving the sale of multiple options — such as short straddles or short strangles — you may want to set a maximum-dollar loss and base your exit point on that, rather than on a specific stock or option price. This approach is commonly used with two-way plays, where more than one element of the strategy can be responsible for a loss. (**Note:** *Portfolio management rules can also play a role in setting loss limits on plays like this, which have unlimited dollar risk. As a rule of thumb, you should never risk more than 5 percent of your account equity on a single play, so that could very well determine the loss limit you'd want to impose on certain strategies.*)

Finally, with some techniques, like covered call writing, the loss limit may be keyed specifically to a downward move in the stock, rather than to a change in the option premium—simply because the stock carries 100 percent of the loss potential in such plays.

We'll talk more about setting precise loss limits—including how to use specialized online trading orders to position them—in just a few minutes. First, however, let's quickly look at the fun side of the exit-strategy equation—the one regarding profit targets.

The Search for Rational Profit Targets

In one sense, setting profit targets for specific option strategies is far easier than establishing loss limits. But, in another, it can be quite complex. As with loss limits, however, one key rule does apply—try to have a sound reason for setting a specific profit target. Don't be totally arbitrary—and don't let your emotions make the decision. To wit, "I *want* to make $2,000 on this play," is **NOT** a sufficiently good reason to set your profit target at $2,000!

Let's first discuss those situations where the issue of a profit target is easily settled. Virtually every strategy that involves the short sale of an option—whether a call or a put—has a maximum potential profit (the exceptions being a few exotic plays such as ratio backspreads). As with losses, however, the optimum result frequently isn't holding out for the absolute maximum. It all depends on the timing.

Take vertical bull or bear spreads, for example. If you initiate a 5-point bull call spread at a net debit of $2.00 a share ($200 per contract), your maximum potential profit at expiration is $3.00 a share, or $300. However, if the underlying stock makes a sharp upmove shortly after you open, putting your short option well in the money, the spread could widen to $4.40 or $4.50 very quickly. The question then becomes: Do you want to grab a quick 120 percent gain (a $240 profit)? Or, do you want hold on for another few weeks in hopes of picking up the final 30 percent ($60), and risk losing it all—and possibly more—should the underlying stock reverse? Unless you're literally consumed with greed, the answer should be obvious: ***Take the money and run!***

As a rule, we recommend taking an early profit on position trades lasting three weeks or more *any time you achieve 80 percent of the potential maximum* (exclusive of commissions) with more than a week remaining until expiration. (If there are only a few days remaining when you hit the 80 percent goal and the spread's well in the money, it may be worth reaching for the last dollar of profit—but only if you're in a position to closely monitor the market.)

Extending that premise, we suggest lowering the target percentage as you shorten the initial lifespan of your spreads and/or increase the volatility of the underlying assets you use. *(**Note:** Volatility is such an important element in option pricing that put and call premiums will sometimes rise even when the underlying stock price doesn't change— simply because overall market volatility increased.)* It's your decision, of course, but you might consider shooting for 70 percent of the maximum on spreads with a two-week horizon, 60 percent on one-week plays and a still-lucrative 50 percent if you try day trading with vertical spreads.

We would apply similar guidelines to limited-profit strategies other than spreads—but with minor modifications. Generally speaking, we advise lowering the target percentage of the maximum profit proportionately as the degree of volatility and the overall level of risk increases. In other words, if you're selling a short strangle on a stock with a fairly modest beta, you might hold out for 70 percent of the potential maximum profit—but if you're day trading naked S&P 500 calls, you should probably be happy if you can keep 25 to 30 percent of the premium you initially receive.

The one exception to this early-out philosophy on short option trades would come when you're writing calls against a long stock position or selling puts against a short stock position. Normally, when doing covered writes, you want to go for the maximum possible profit on the option, which you will get either when it expires worthless or when it's exercised (or you buy it back right before expiration if you want to keep the stock). The only time you settle for less is when you close out the entire position early in order to cut off a loss caused by an adverse move in the price of the underlying stock. (*NOTE: Another alternative in such circumstances is to "roll" your short option position up or down — i.e., buying back the option you were originally short and selling another with a higher or lower striking price, depending on how the underlying security has moved. Because of the high number of variables involved, we won't offer specific guidelines for "rolling" a position, but you should be aware of this possible strategy alternative if you plan to be an active trader.)*

A Trickier Exercise in Target Setting

Setting profit targets on strategies that don't impose a potential maximum requires a little more thought and planning. As it was with the actual selection of strategies (see Key Step 3), a key consideration in setting targets is the nature of the underlying asset you're using — particularly its volatility.

To illustrate, assume it's late January and JKL stock is trading at $24 a share. You think the market is likely to advance over the next couple of months, taking JKL stock with it. So, you buy a March 25 JKL call with a premium of $1.00 — or $100 for the full contract. Obviously, with an outright call purchase, there's no strategic limit on the potential gain — so where do you set your profit target? Unfortunately, with so little information, it's really impossible to say.

To remedy this situation, you first need to project how large a move you think the market will make. Then, based on JKL's beta, you need to estimate how well it might track the market. If you assume the market's going to rise by 15 percent, and the JKL stock has a beta of 0.90, then you could expect it to gain around 13.5 percent. Apply that to the current price of $24, and you'd get a target price for the stock of around $27.25 — which would give the March 25 call an intrinsic value of $2.25. Even assuming a fairly rapid upmove, which would leave the call with a fair amount of time value, the most you could thus expect the option to be worth would be around $2.75. Subtract the original cost of $1.00 from that, and you'd get a maximum probable profit of $1.75—or $175 on the full contract. Given that, it would make absolutely no sense to set a profit target of $300 on this particular speculation—but $150 per contract might be quite reasonable.

That's the kind of thought process you have to apply in setting profit targets for option strategies that have theoretically unlimited potential. Of course, every situation is different. For example, given the exact same situation listed above, a profit target of $300 might have made sense for, say, a March 25 Dell Computer call—simply because Dell has a beta of 2.19, not 0.90 (though the initial premium for a Dell call would likely have been higher than $1.00). There are also numerous other considerations that may factor in, ranging from the stock's recent trading pattern, its current trend and resistance or support levels to fundamental elements such as earnings expectations or seasonal sales patterns.

Obviously, the process gets more streamlined with shorter-term trades and higher-volatility assets, simply because there's less time in which various factors can have an impact. Still, even day traders need to apply sound logic to their trading goals. For example, it would make no sense to set a profit target on an index put that would require the S&P 100 to drop 15 points at a time when the largest one-day decline by the Index in two months had been just 10 points. And, it would be equally irrational to target a two-point profit on an S&P 500 call when the Index had been routinely making single-day advances of eight and nine points.

(Note: Once again, we have taken a procedure that can be fairly simple and made it seem overly complicated for the sake of illustration. In practice, you will most likely avail yourself of one of the integrated trading partners offered by your online broker, using their software to do much of the target-setting analysis for you. In fact, with some of the more sophisticated option services now available, you can simply specify the underlying asset you want to trade and the computer will identify the best potential option choices, run "what-if" scenarios and project potential profit targets— which you can readily adopt as your own.)

The target-setting error on the S&P 500 call serves as the perfect lead-in for a subject we mentioned earlier—giving yourself a little "wiggle room" when it comes to taking profits. While it is indeed important to set a target on every trade you open—and equally important to grab those targeted gains on plays with a maximum profit limit—you probably shouldn't take your profits the instant your target is reached on an open-ended speculation. Instead, you should try to extend your winning run, while protecting your existing gains through the use of stops and other specialized trading orders—which is far easier to do as an online trader than it ever was through a conventional broker.

Using Stops and Limit Orders

You got a preview of specialized online orders in Key Step 3 when we talked about opening and closing positions using contingent-on-stock and stop-on-stock orders. In the remainder of this Step, we'll discuss both adding to and protecting your option profits using limit orders and stop orders keyed to the actual option price.

As with the two types of conditional orders, option stop orders and option limit orders are essentially the opposite of one another. Each can be used with options on a variety of underlying assets, including both individual stocks and market indexes. Depending on your precise objective, each can also be utilized to either open or close option trades. To clarify, here's a brief summary of exactly how you can employ these orders in varying situations:

- An *opening* limit order can be used to *BUY* either a call or a put for a specified price *at or below the current level.*

- An *opening* limit order can be used to *SELL SHORT* either a call or a put for a specified price *at or above the current level.*

- A *closing* limit order can be used to *SELL* (take profits on) either a long call or a long put for a specified price *at or above the current level.*

- A *closing* limit order can be used to *BUY BACK* (take profits on) either a short call or a short put for a specified price *at or below the current level.*

- An *opening* stop order can be used to *BUY* either a call or a put if the option's price *rises to a specific level.*

- An *opening* stop order can be used to *SELL SHORT* either a call or a put if the option's price *falls to a specific level.*

- A *closing* stop order can be used to *SELL* (protect profits on) either a long call or a long put if the option's price *falls to a specified level.*

- A *closing* stop order can be used to *BUY BACK* (protect profits on) either a short call or a short put if the option's price *rises to a specified level.*

Like orders that are conditional on stock price movements, stop and limit orders based on the actual option prices provide a broad spectrum of strategic alternatives. However, they're primarily used to limit losses, to protect or increase profits on winning trades and to garner better prices on perceived market opportunities. For example, if you're long puts on the Nasdaq Composite Index, and the market shows signs of turning higher, you can enter a "stop sell close" order that will activate and cut off your losses should the price of the puts fall to a specified level below their current market price.

Similarly, if you've got a nice profit on a bull call spread and the underlying stock starts to turn lower, you can take profits on your long call, but keep the short call, placing a "stop buy close" order slightly above its current price. If the underlying stock continues to fall, the short call price will also decline and your stop won't be triggered, thus allowing you to cover later at a better price. However, if the underlying stock turns higher again, the stop will activate and your short call will be covered, cutting off your potential loss. (Note: "Legging out" of the long side of spread in this fashion will likely trigger a sizable margin call, so strategies such as this may be restricted to traders with larger accounts.)

Limit orders can also be used to take profits—but *only* when you're trying to enlarge an existing gain. In other words, you'd enter a "limit sell close" order if you were long a call or put and wanted to exit at a price higher than the current premium level (or if you were short a call or put and wanted to close at a lower price level). As such, they're generally more effective as a tool for opening new trades. Specifically, you might use a limit order to trigger the purchase of a call (or put) should the price fall to a more reasonable level—or to initiate a short call (or put) position if the premium increased to a more attractive level. In either situation, you'd enter the option price you wanted, and the order would activate only when the option actually traded at that price.

Limit and stop orders can be entered on either a "day" or "good-till-canceled" basis—and they can be revoked at any time. *(**Note:** A "day" order, if not filled by 4 p.m. Eastern time, when the major markets close, is automatically cancelled after the final bell.)* You cannot, however, change the stop or limit price on a pending order. Instead, you have to cancel the pending order and then re-enter it with the new price—or as a regular market order. This latter tactic is often used by traders trying to "leg into" spreads or other combinations—e.g., they'll try to get a fill at a desired limit

One Warning on Stop and Contingent Orders

If you're considering stop or contingent orders, it's important for you be aware of the actual mechanics that make them work. With the advent of ECNs, individual options may be traded on more than one—or even all five—of the U.S. option exchanges. If an order is entered with a stop, that stop is triggered only when the specified price is reached on *all* exchanges. (This is referred to as the "consolidated quote.") As a result, an option contract might be bid or offered at the stop level on one exchange, yet not be triggered because a better price exists on another exchange. For stop orders based on a stock or index price, the underlying security's last trade triggers the option order.

Be aware, as well, that a simple stop order won't guarantee the stop price. A trade at the stop price merely triggers entry of the order; it doesn't fill it. And, in a highly volatile market, the price could move above (on a buy stop) or below (on a sell stop) the desired price. Stops contingent on a stock or index may also be "missed" if a sudden market shift causes a "gap" move in the price of the underlying security, thereby resulting in a fill at prices substantially different from that specified. Two other key points:

1. A "stop-loss order" converts to **a market order** once the specified price has been reached. However, if the order is to sell, the stop price must be "bid"—and, if the order is to buy, the stop price must be the "offered" or "asked" price.

2. A "stop-limit order" converts to **a limit order** once the specified price has been reached. Therefore, if a second "bid" or "offer" isn't available at the same price or better, the limit order won't be executed.

or stop price for most of the trading session, then switch to a market order shortly before the close in order to complete their position. Alternately, having failed to complete the combination, they may cancel the limit or stop order and use a market order to close the "leg" that was opened earlier in the day.

As you can thus see, the potential variations — and profit opportunities — are virtually endless with stop and limit orders. And, as with orders conditional on the price of the underlying stock or index, placing stop and limit orders based on option prices is quite easy with the order-entry software provided by the top online brokers. To illustrate, let's check out a couple of quick examples.

A Couple of Sample Orders

Assume it's early September and, even though it's fairly choppy right now, you think the market is likely to rally prior to the expiration of the September options. You also like the outlook for Dell Computer, which last traded at $25 a share, and think it might be a good stock with which to play coming advance.

However, you're not at all happy with the prices of the Dell calls, particularly the September 25 contracts, which are currently offered at $2.50 — at least half a dollar above what you'd like to pay.

Normally in such a situation, you'd just bide your time and hope to catch a market dip, during which you could quickly place an order at a lower price. However, you can't do that today because you have to leave for a business meeting and won't be able to watch the market. What do you do? Simple. You merely place *a limit order* to "Buy Open" 10 Dell September 25 calls at a price of $2.00. You type in the specifics of the order, as shown in Figure 4-1 on page 81, press the "Send" button and, in a few seconds, the potential trade appears on your "Working" orders screen, identified with its own order number and the time of entry. Satisfied, you head off to your meeting.

Later in the day, you return from your meeting, quickly log on to your online brokerage account and check the status of your order. Sure enough, the market did go through some fairly large gyrations during the day, with Dell slipping to $23.85 at one point. On the

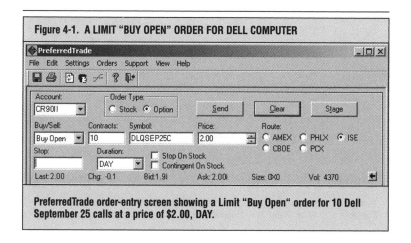

Figure 4-1. A LIMIT "BUY OPEN" ORDER FOR DELL COMPUTER

PreferredTrade order-entry screen showing a Limit "Buy Open" order for 10 Dell September 25 calls at a price of $2.00, DAY.

pullback, your limit order for the Dell September 25 calls was triggered and filled at your desired price of $2.00. Content, you sit back and wait for the market to rally in the days to come—which it does.

Indeed, over the next week-and-a-half, Dell's stock rises to $32—with every indication it could go higher still, since it penetrated a resistance level at $31.25. Your September 25 Dell calls, for which you paid $2.00, are now bid at $7.50, giving you a substantial dollar profit of $5,500 on your 10-contract position. Since you think the rally may continue, you'd like to play for an even larger gain—but, with only four days remaining until expiration, you don't want to risk the profits you have. What do you do? Again, the answer is simple. Rather than having to constantly monitor Dell's price action, you merely enter *a stop order* to "Sell Close" 10 Dell September 25 calls should the bid price fall to, say, $6.50, as shown in Figure 4-2 on page 82. Again, you press the "Send" button and, a few seconds later, your protective stop is in place.

The next day, Dell climbs to $33.80 and the bid on your September 25 calls rises to $8.90, so you cancel your current stop order and enter a new one with a stop price of $8.15 (this process is referred to as using a "trailing stop")—thereby reducing your potential give-back amount to $750. The following day, Dell opens flat—

Figure 4-2. A STOP "SELL CLOSE" ORDER FOR DELL COMPUTER

PreferredTrade order-entry screen showing a Stop "Sell Close" order for 10 Dell September 25 calls, based on a stop price of $6.50, GTC.

and, though your stop hasn't been hit, you decide to exit and avoid the potential volatility associated with the September "triple-witching hour." You cancel your working stop, quickly re-enter a market order to "Sell Close"—and, in less than a minute, sit happily contemplating what you're going to do with your profits.

A Quick Summary

Like orders conditional on stock prices, limit orders can't be applied in all situations—but stops can be used with virtually every option strategy you employ. They can get you into trades you might otherwise miss, get you out of trades when things turn against you, and limit your losses or preserve your profits when you're wrong. However, you can't blindly rely on stops to get you out of every trade. You still have to plan, think and make decisions about when—or if—you should use a stop, and where to place it. And, as with all orders, you have to concentrate on what you're doing to ensure you enter them correctly. To help in that respect, here's a quick recap regarding the use of both stop and limit orders based on option prices:

• **Limit orders** (with no stop price) to *BUY* are used when you want to purchase a put or call *AT or BELOW* the current market price of the option.

Some Notes on Placing Your Stops

As with loss limits and profit targets, exact placement of your "stop price" also requires some thought. It will typically represent a combination of your own preference regarding how much of your profit you want to risk giving back, plus any technical factors you may be aware of. In the Dell example, putting the stop at an option price of $6.50 reflected a willingness to give up $1,000 of the $5,500 profit, and also corresponded to a pullback in the price of the Dell stock to roughly $31.25, the resistance level it had earlier breached. Obviously, circumstances will be different for each stop you enter, so we can't provide firm placement rules. However, we can offer some guidelines:

- If your profit is fairly small, keep the stop fairly tight; you don't want to let your gain turn into a loss.

- The more volatile the underlying asset, the larger the cushion between the current price and your stop should be. Put the stop too tight and you could get "whipsawed" — i.e., robbed of what would have been a large profit because you were knocked out on a brief price dip.

- Tighten your stop as you near your anticipated exit date or the option's expiration approaches. You don't want to work three or four weeks building a profit, then lose most of it in the final couple of days.

- Pay attention to upcoming economic events that could affect your trade. For example, if you're riding a bullish trade, but you suspect the market may react negatively to next Tuesday's Federal Reserve meeting, you may want to either tighten your stop — or go ahead and close entirely. After all, why slavishly rely on a stop and almost certainly give back hundreds of dollars when you can just as easily avoid the expected reversal altogether.

- **Limit orders** (with no stop price) to *SELL* are used when you want to sell a put or call AT or ABOVE the current market price of the option.

- **Stop orders** to *BUY* are placed when you want to purchase a put or call at a specific price *ABOVE* the current market price of the option.

- **Stop orders** to *SELL* are placed when you want to sell a put or call at a specific price *BELOW* the current market price of the option.

In addition, there are two types of option stop orders, distinguished as follows:

- **Stop-Market Orders** convert to *a market order* — to either buy or sell — once the specified stop price is reached. The order will then be executed at the best-available price.

- **Stop-Limit Orders** convert to *a limit order* to buy (or sell) at a specified price once a trade occurs at the designated stop price. The order will then be executed at the limit price (or better), unless no identical offer (or bid) exists at that time, in which case the order may not be filled. (Note: With stop-limit *buy* orders, the limit price may be no more than *$1.00 above* the stop price, and with stop-limit *sell* orders, the limit price may be no more than *$1.00 below* the stop price.)

With those important points clarified regarding the use of stop and limit orders in planning and implementing your exit strategies, let's now move ahead and look at some of the other issues you'll have to address when trading options online.

Chapter 5

KEY STEP NO. 5:
Don't Let the Details Defeat You

To this point, we've painted a fairly rosy picture of how well the online trading process works and how easy it is to perform most of the necessary functions. In the interests of fairness, however, we must admit that you **WILL** occasionally run into some minor complications—or even modest problems. We must also warn that, because online trading technology is really still in its infancy, you'll almost certainly encounter a number of things you're not able to do. Finally, as with any investment endeavor, you'll still have to deal with all the government regulations, account requirements, exchange rules, established trading procedures and other general market minutiae. There's simply no way around these petty irritations.

The important thing, if you want to be successful, is to not let these details defeat you. View them as necessary evils, and deal with them calmly when they arise—all the while keeping your primary focus on the market and your actual trading activity. Of course, the secret to calmly handling details is to understand and anticipate them—which is what this Key Step will help you do.

Starting at the Top

We'll talk about how to pick the best online broker in Key Step No. 7. However, regardless of the firm you decide to use, your first two steps will be the same—opening the account and installing the online trading software.

While there will be some minor differences in the account forms, they'll all be essentially the same, requiring you to enter basic biographical and financial data as mandated by the firm, the exchanges and the SEC. As a result, we won't waste much time talking about them. Just be sure to read everything carefully before signing — including the small print, which spells out the firm's liability to you and your responsibilities to the firm, and to other traders. In reality, there are only about three potential hang-ups with respect to opening an account: Some firms require a higher degree of investing experience before allowing option trading; some have higher net-worth (suitability) requirements for option clients; and some require larger opening deposits to set up the account. (At the very least, you'll have to put up $5,000 — and some firms require minimums of $25,000 or more.) One other item you may want to check is whether the firm observes the exchange-minimum margin requirement on short and combination option plays — or if they're more conservative and want a higher security bond on certain types of trades.

Variations in procedure, with respect to the trading software, are somewhat broader. Some firms have websites and let you download the software directly; some with, and some without, a special code. Others send the software out on disk or CD-ROM and you install from there, making your online connection only after the program's up and running. Some trading software is highly sophisticated, with lots of choices you can make, and some is so simple your grandmother can use it successfully on the first try. (We would have said, "your kids can use it," but today's kids can *always* figure out new software, instantly.) In either case, our advice is the same as with the account forms — read everything completely and carefully.

Study the documentation carefully; check out what's available in the "Help" file; find and make note of the e-mail address and phone number of the broker's technical-support service (and the hours it's open); and walk through the demo if the program (or the broker's website) has one. Once you've done that, check out the available online resources the software provides, calling up some stock quotes, option quotes, index readings, charts, news, etc. — whatever the program offers. Check out the availability of integrated trading partners you might want to use for research, analysis and screening—or, if you've already signed up for one, make sure you understand the various functions you can perform with the service and exactly how its software interacts with that of your brokerage firm.

Finally, identify the four or five option strategies you'll likely be using most often and try a few dry runs. Fill in the order-entry screen for an option purchase and a short sale; for a spread or a staged combination. Use a contingent order or a stop order; a limit-buy or limit-sell. Fill in all the contract specifics and designate the order parameters—right up to the point of hitting the "Send" button or releasing the staged orders. (To stay on the safe side, you may want to practice with orders that have no chance of being filled—say buying an IBM 25 call with a price of 75 cents.) Before you clear each practice order, review it carefully to ensure you did everything correctly. It's better to discover some mistake you're making, now, then when you're urgently trying to enter a real order—with real money on the line!

Some Potential Problem Areas

Once you're ready to actually start trading—entering real orders—there are a couple of places where you're likely to run into trouble. One is entering the wrong specifications for the option you want to trade—e.g., the wrong symbol, price code, month code or option type (put or call). The other is trying to do something that's either not allowed or that the software isn't technologically capable of doing.

With respect to the former problem, the symbol issue can be quite confusing because many Nasdaq-listed issues have different symbols for the options and the underlying stock itself. Fortunately, the better online brokerage software packages include remedies for that and other entry-specification concerns. For example, the PreferredTrade package I use lets you request a chain of option quotes simply by typing in the stock symbol, the month(s) you want and the strike-price range you're interested in. The resulting display will show the option symbol, even if it's different from that of the stock, as well as the month codes and the strike-price designations, with calls and puts situated on opposite sides of the screen. (Refer back to Figure 2-1 in Chapter 2: Key Step No. 2 for an example.)

In addition, with the PreferredTrade software, you don't really have to type in the option specifications yourself. You can simply click on the option you want in the pricing table you've called up—or on the analysis screen of one of the integrated trading partners—and the software will automatically transfer that option, properly coded, to the "Symbol" field on the order-entry screen. Then, all you have to do is specify whether you are buying or selling; fill in the number of contracts, the desired price and any stop or limit restrictions—and press "Send" (or "Stage," if that's the case).

Likewise, you don't have to type anything when you want to cancel an order. You merely click on the item you want in the "Working Orders" field, and it will be displayed in the order-entry area; then, just press "Clear" and it will be canceled. **(Note:** *Until a cancel is confirmed, the order is still a working order and may be executed.)*

Obviously, that makes life pretty simple when placing option orders through PreferredTrade—but, just in case you're using a broker with less helpful software, we've provided the standard option month and strike-price codes in Figure 5-1 on page 89.

Learning to Live With the Rules

Unfortunately, dealing with issues related to exchange rules or technological weaknesses aren't so easily overcome. We've already mentioned a few of the potential problems with rules in earlier steps—including the prohibition on stop-limit orders with limits more than $1.00 away from the present market price and the requirement that stops be activated only by the "consolidated quote," which may result in a stop not being triggered as expected.

There are a number of other similar restrictions, and some of them —like high margin requirements—will no doubt inconvenience you or restrict your strategic opportunities. However, there's no sense letting it frustrate you. Remember, rules are just that—rules. Barring government intervention or an overwhelming investor (or industry) revolt, they're not likely to change. Thus, all you can do is learn what they are—and then abide by them.

Figure 5-1. OPTION MONTH AND STRIKE-PRICE CODES

OPTION MONTH CODES

Month	Calls	Puts	Month	Calls	Puts
January	A	M	July	G	S
February	B	N	August	H	T
March	C	O	September	I	U
April	D	P	October	J	V
May	E	Q	November	K	W
June	F	R	December	L	X

OPTION PRICE CODES

Strike Prices	Code	Strike Prices	Code	Strike Prices	Code
5, 105, 205, 305, 405	A	55, 155, 255, 355, 455	K	7.5, 37.5, 67.5, 97.5	U
10, 110, 210, 310, 410	B	60, 160, 260, 360, 460	L	12.5, 42.5, 72.5, 102.5	V
15, 115, 215, 315, 415	C	65, 165, 265, 365, 465	M	17.5, 47.5, 77.5, 107.5	W
20, 120, 220, 320, 420	D	70, 170, 270, 370, 470	N	22.5, 52.5, 82.5, 112.5	X
25, 125, 225, 325, 425	E	75, 175, 275, 375, 475	O	27.5, 57.5, 87.5, 117.5	Y
30, 130, 230, 330, 430	F	80, 180, 280, 380, 480	P	32.5, 62.5, 92.5, 122.5	Z
35, 135, 235, 335, 435	G	85, 185, 285, 385, 485	Q		
40, 140, 240, 340, 440	H	90, 190, 290, 390, 490	R		
45, 145, 245, 345, 445	I	95, 195, 295, 395, 495	S		
50, 150, 250, 350, 450	J	100, 200, 300, 400, 500	T		

One set of rules you particularly need to pay attention to relates to the procedures for exercising options at expiration — or, on rare occasions, prior to expiration. For starters, the rules of the Options Clearing Corporation (OCC) dictate that stock options that are less than 75 cents ($0.75) in the money will **NOT** be automatically exercised. If you want your broker to exercise an equity option with an intrinsic value of 74 cents or less at expiration, you must specifically instruct him to do so. Absent such instructions, the option will expire worthless — just as if it were out of the money. You must also be timely in issuing your exercise instructions; they have to reach the broker by 4:45 p.m., Eastern time, on the final trading day before expiration.

Instructions aren't required for options that are 75 cents or more in the money, as OCC rules mandate their automatic exercise. However, whether automatic or manual, the act of exercising an option creates several responsibilities for you as the owner of a long call or put. If you're exercising an index option, the process is fairly simple because they are "cash settled"—meaning your account is simply credited or debited for the option's monetary value (which is based on the closing index level on the final trading day of the expiration cycle). But, if you are exercising a stock option, things get a bit more complicated. You must have the necessary cash to pay for the stock if you're exercising a call—and you must own the stock to deliver if you're exercising a put. A failure on either count will result in what is called a "Reg T call"—a demand that you instantly come up with the cash, or stock, needed to fulfill your obligation. (**Note:** When you buy an option, you buy a *right*—but, the instant you exercise the option, that right is converted into an *obligation*, which *must* be met.)

Likewise, if you are short an option and it is exercised against you, you must have either the cash to buy the stock underlying your short put, or the underlying stock to deliver to satisfy your short call (or the cash to buy it for later delivery). Once again, insufficient liquidity on your part will prompt a Reg T margin call. If you fail to meet such a call within the required time, your broker will then have the right to liquidate any other positions in your account to raise the necessary cash—even if such a liquidation might cause significant losses.

Thus, the prime rule with respect to exercising options is this: Make *absolutely* sure you have enough cash on hand to cover your obligations. If you don't—or think last-minute price changes might make it unlikely—you shouldn't even consider getting involved in the exercise process. Instead, sell or buy back your in-the-money options prior to expiration. That's the only sure way to offset your pending obligation. (In fact, only around 5 percent of all in-the-money options are exercised; the other 95 percent are offset with closing purchases or sales.)

A Couple of Procedural Items

There are a few potential sources of unexpected inconvenience or irritation that aren't really rule-related, as much as linked to either brokerage or exchange procedures. For example:

Fast-market conditions—Most of the time, the option-routing functions of the ECNs and the automatic order fulfillment systems at the exchanges work in a timely and efficient manner, just as we've described. However, when trading really heats up and volume climbs dramatically—a so-called "fast market"—the systems, and the people, may get overwhelmed. When that happens, excess order-flow may be arbitrarily routed away from the automatic systems and into the public-order books at the exchanges. This can result in lengthy delays on limit orders, especially those well away from the market, and slow processing of market orders. Fast-market conditions can also lead to misdirected orders, incomplete fills, executions at poor prices and delays in reporting trade results.

The exchange and brokerage systems are steadily getting better at handling these situations—but volume also keeps increasing, so it's an ongoing battle. Thus, you shouldn't be surprised by an occasional fast market. (**Note:** As the small print we mentioned earlier when talking about your account forms will explain, your broker has *no liability* if your option orders don't get executed—even under fast-market conditions. It's your sole responsibility to protect yourself against over-exposure to risk in such circumstances.)

Stop-order processing—Some online brokers simply pass your stop and limit orders on to the exchanges, letting the responsibility for recognizing and honoring the stop and limit prices fall on the floor traders—who may, or may not, give such orders their full attention. Other brokers, who place more emphasis on options, may hold the stops in-house, where their options desk will monitor them, releasing them into the automatic system only when they're triggered. This is a better system because it prevents stops from being activated by bad ticks, after-hours trades or other pricing irregularities. If your broker is really option oriented, the firm's software will automatically "validate" your stop and limit orders, ensuring their relationship to the current market price is correct—and provide warning messages on your screen if they're not. A sophisticated program, like that provided by PreferredTrade, will even review limit prices and suggest how you might adjust them to improve the likelihood of an execution.

Good-till-canceled order processing—As noted earlier, GTC orders can be used for most of your online trades. However, GTC stop or contingent orders will *not* be executed during the first round of daily trades (the so-called "opening rotation") on an exchange. That round of trades is used to generate quotes, which are then disseminated by the exchange as a trigger for both new stops and limits, as well as held-over GTC stop or contingent orders—which may then be executed if the price is appropriate. As already noted, GTC orders can also be affected negatively if the underlying stock or index changes significantly in value overnight, resulting in a "gap opening" (either up or down). In such instances, GTC limit orders may not get filled and GTC market orders or stop-market orders may be filled at substantially worse prices than expected.

Nasdaq stop exclusions—Currently, GTC stop orders are not allowed on Nasdaq stocks. Only "day" stops are permitted.

The Technology Keeps Improving

While there's little chance that irritations related to rules or procedures will be alleviated, hope springs eternal when it comes to beneficial upgrades in online trading technology. Much of the software that allows efficient online trading wasn't even on the drawing boards as little as five years ago, so nobody in the industry—even the brokers who've been around since the beginning—has what could truly be called "a finished product." As a result, while it's now fairly easy to accomplish everything you really *need* to be a successful online trader, you probably won't be able to do everything you'd like—or do it in exactly the way you want.

Take trading orders, for example. The securities industry probably recognizes close to 20 different types of orders—ranging from simple market and limit orders to such specialized entries as "fill-or-kill," "immediate-or-cancel" and "market-on-close" orders. Since we've already covered the full range of available online option orders, it should be obvious you're pretty much out of luck if you want one of those exotic numbers. But do you really need them? Probably not.

Unfortunately, the same can't be said for the capability to position multiple-option strategies using a single order. While many of the better online order-entry systems now let you order vertical bull and bear spreads as a single package (with a single commission), only a few accept unit orders for straddles or strangles. And virtually none will take single orders for horizontal (calendar) spreads or complex strategies like ratio back-spreads, condors or butterflies. However, every software tech in the industry is working to resolve these shortcomings, and new features appear with every program upgrade. Thus, by the time you read this, you may already be able to do some of the things we just said you couldn't.

Most online order-entry programs also reject so-called "combination orders" — which are attempts to simultaneously perform two different ordering functions with a single entry. For example, some traders will try to place a buy order for an option and, at the same time, enter a stop to protect that option once it's purchased. They'll enter a limit in the "Price" field of the order-entry screen, and then put a much lower stop price in the "Stop" field, press "Send" and think both orders are working when, in fact, they'll both be rejected. To make this process work, you must first enter a limit "Buy Open" order for the option. Then, when you get a fill, you go back and enter a stop order to protect your position.

Coming Soon — "Order Cancels Order"

Another feature that's presently missing from most systems — but which will likely become available in the next round of upgrades — is the ability to set up an "order-cancels-order" arrangement. This will be a valuable innovation for both day traders and position traders — though they may have slightly different objectives in utilizing it.

What occurs with an order-cancels-order (OCO) arrangement is this: You put one stop order above the current market price and another stop order of the same type below the current market price. Both orders work until one is filled, at which point the other is automatically canceled.

As the electronic trading system presently stands, you can have two buy orders working on the same option at the same time, but you can have only one sell order working on any given option at one time — unless you are a "qualified investor" who has approval and is willing to sell options short. The reasoning behind these restrictions is purely a matter of risk control, explained as follows:

If you have two stop-buy orders entered and the market (or stock price) moves so fast that both get filled before you have a chance to cancel the second one, your resulting risk is still contained—limited to the total premium you paid for the two positions. Plus, you can turn right around and place a market sell order to close one of the positions—usually with only a small loss. But, if you have two sell orders working at the same time, the outcome can be far different. Presumably, you would have the sell orders in because you had an open long position. The first sell order to be executed would thus close your long option—but, if the market moved so fast that the second sell order was also filled before you could cancel it, you would be left with a naked short position. And, as you already know, that carries essentially unlimited risk (not to mention a hefty margin requirement). Thus, if the market continued a rapid adverse move—and it was a while before you noticed your mistake or were able to cover—you could suffer a potentially devastating loss.

However, "order cancels order" ends all that. If you have two buy orders in and one is filled, the second automatically cancels—leaving you with a single long position. Likewise, if you have two sell orders in and one is filled, the second automatically cancels, leaving you with no position at all—and no risk exposure. A substantially different outcome from the present situation—and much to your benefit.

So, assuming OCO is indeed the next online trading innovation, how might you use it? For position traders, the answer is clear—OCO is an ideal tool for protecting existing profits on a long option position, while simultaneously paving the way to potentially larger gains. To clarify how that would work, let's revisit the Dell Computer example we used near the end of Key Step 4 (see pages 81-82), when we talked about stop orders.

If you'll recall, the trader in that case purchased 10 September 25 Dell calls at a price of $2.00 when Dell's stock slipped below $24 a share on an intra-day basis. Dell then rallied over the next couple of weeks, climbing to $32 a share—which lifted the option premium to $7.50 bid, producing a profit of $5,500 on the 10-contract position with just four days left until expiration. Assuming once again that you were that trader, your stated goal at that point was to play for an even larger gain—but without risking the profits you already had. To do that, you had to protect yourself by entering a buy-stop order at a call price of $6.50, while also diligently watching the market for an upmove that might let you take a larger profit.

That's an adequate plan—but it has one flaw. If you have something else to do, or merely get distracted, you could miss the upmove—particularly amid the increased volatility leading up to a triple-witching hour. If that happened, you might not only forfeit the hoped-for extra profit, but also see the option price fall back to your stop—wiping out $1,000 of your current gain. However, with an order-cancels-order arrangement, you rid yourself of those worries—as well as the need to monitor the market every minute. With OCO, you merely place *two* good-till-canceled sell-stop orders—one at an option price of $6.50, your stop-loss point, and the other at $8.75, your hoped-for target for taking larger profits.

The next day, Dell climbs to $33.80 (as it did in the earlier example) and the closing bid on your September 25 calls rises to $8.90. This time, however, you don't have to either raise your stop-loss or worry about what's going to happen the next day. Why? Because the upper sell-stop order in your OCO configuration was triggered—automatically cashing in your added profits and, at the same time, canceling the lower stop-loss sell order. It's that simple.

Of course, had Dell made a smaller move and the stop not been triggered, you would have still had the option to cancel both orders and re-enter them with new stop prices. Or, had Dell been flat that day, you could have simply left them in place. Finally, had you so desired, you could have opted to exit "manually"—canceling both sell-stop orders and entering a "Sell Close" order at the market. In other words, with OCO you have just as much flexibility, but with fewer worries and more opportunity.

Day traders can use an OCO configuration in the same fashion—except, of course, they'll use "day" rather than GTC orders, their trades will likely involve index options rather than stock options and the spreads between their designated prices will likely be smaller (a reflection of the higher "multipliers" for most indexes). However, day traders can also use OCO combinations as entry triggers if they don't like the prices they see when the market first opens. For example, a bearish trader might place two buy-stops for index puts—one above the opening price and one below. The actual placement points (or stop prices) could be based on technical considerations, such as at perceived resistance or support levels, on pricing instincts or merely as a function of bargain hunting.

If one of the buy stops were triggered, the other would cancel. The trader could then position OCO sell-stops above and below the long put's market price, instantly establishing both a loss limit and a target price for the day trade. And, if neither stop were triggered, the trader would merely remain out of the market that day—having failed to find an option priced to his liking.

Given these potential advantages, the OCO feature will obviously be a welcome addition to your broker's order-entry program—as will many of the other technical improvements we've discussed. However, rather than sitting here and waiting for the next round of software upgrades, let's move ahead to Key Step No. 6 and review some important money-management considerations.

Chapter 6

KEY STEP NO. 6:
It's Real Money, So Manage It

Options trading can be extremely fast paced—particularly in the online environment. As you've already seen, it offers tremendous leverage and exceptional profit potential—but it also carries sizeable risks. As such, it has many of the same elements as gambling, and many traders develop something of a "high roller" attitude—frequently to their detriment. However, the dollars in your online options trading account aren't gaming chips. They're real money—and they should be managed accordingly.

Failure to properly apportion and control your capital—i.e., to manage your money based on a well-thought-out plan—is a major stumbling block on the road to financial success, regardless of the investments involved. However, with options, OTC stocks, futures or any other high-risk vehicle, lack of clear goals and precise strategic objectives can be a formula for disaster. Indeed, if you operate in a knee-jerk fashion, being reactive rather than proactive, the list of mistakes you can make is virtually endless. These include:

• Trading based on emotion rather than fact, which can lead to irrational (or even hysterical) decisions—and devastating losses.

• Trading too much, thereby reducing the quality of your positions and increasing commissions and other costs.

• Initiating trades for which you're not mentally suited—i.e., trades that keep you awake at night.

• Using strategies you really don't understand—then being surprised by the unanticipated outcome.

- Taking profits too soon—and hanging on to losers too long.

- Losing too much, too soon, on too few trades, thereby leaving yourself with insufficient capital to make a later recovery.

- Taking advice from the wrong people, including the "talking heads" on TV who have an "instant analysis" for every little market move.

Fortunately, if you start out with a solid plan, then do your homework before (and during) your trades, you can avoid most of these mistakes in your online trading endeavors.

Obviously, we can't look inside your mind and gauge your emotional state, nor can we accurately evaluate your individual financial situation. Thus, as was the case when we talked about setting loss limits, we won't attempt to give you a precise personal money-management plan. What we will do, however, is offer some widely accepted guidelines for managing assets in speculative accounts.

The first of these guidelines relates to the actual size of your online account. As we've repeatedly emphasized, trading options—even with the most conservative strategies—is essentially pure speculation. Most financial experts recommend that you devote no more than *10 to 15 percent* of your total investment capital *to speculation*—and, then, only when the value of your portfolio has reached a minimum of $50,000, with $100,000 preferred. Given this, if you can't put up—and afford to lose—at least $5,000 to $15,000, you shouldn't even consider trading options. (Most brokers won't even let you open an account for less than $5,000—and some require as much as $25,000.) You can, of course, increase the amount dedicated to speculation as your portfolio grows, but those same experts suggest a speculative cap of around $200,000, regardless of how much wealth you have.

Allocating Your Trading Funds

Once you've funded your online trading account, the question then becomes: "How do I allocate my money among various trades?" The next two guidelines provide the answer:

First, never risk more than *5 to 10 percent* of your total account equity on *a single trade*. In other words, if you have $20,000 with which to work, don't implement any strategy that has a risk in excess of $1,000 to $2,000. If you have a smaller account, this means you'll probably be limited to the purchase of calls or puts on stocks, or to limited-risk plays such as vertical bull and bear spreads. You probably won't be able to trade many index options, simply because the premiums—and thus the risks—tend to be quite a bit larger. (**Note:** If you do open trades with higher maximum risks, these loss limits should be a prime consideration in determining where to set protective stops.)

On the other hand, if you have a $150,000 account, you will be able to risk $7,500 to $15,000 per trade—which means you'll be able to do virtually anything, including selling "naked" options if you have the temperament for it.

Once you decide how much money to risk on a single trade, the next step is to determine how many positions you should have open at any given time—or, by association, how much of your account equity should be committed to option trades at any one time. The accepted rule is: Limit your *total option exposure* to no *more than 60 percent* of your account value—with 50 percent actually preferred. Thus, if you have $10,000 in your account, you should have no more than $6,000 tied up in trades or margin requirements—and $5,000 would be better. Coupled with the single-trade limit, that would mean you should have no more than five to six trades open at any given time. (Actually, given the flood of financial information now available via TV and the Internet, that's probably as many underlying assets as you can reasonably expect to follow, anyway.)

Why Follow the Guidelines

If you're the aggressive type, you may think those guidelines are too restrictive. "After all," you might say, "we are talking about speculation here, so why be so conservative?"

If we wanted to be flip, we could respond, "Better conservative, than broke"—and, actually, ensuring you don't go broke is one of the reasons to follow these guidelines. By setting your per-trade and equity-commitment limits as we've suggested you accomplish several important money-management goals:

1. You virtually eliminate the possibility of losing the entire amount with which you opened your account—or, for "naked" short sellers, even more.

2. You ensure that there is always sufficient reserve capital in your account to protect against short-term adverse price movements that might cause a margin call.

3. You guarantee that, even if you suffer three or four consecutive losses, you will still have a large enough capital base to continue trading—and recoup your losses on your next winning streak.

4. Finally, you increase your sense of security—assuring a mental attitude that lets you play from a position of strength, rather than succumbing to fear and making emotional trading decisions.

Thus, our contention is, while it's all right to be somewhat aggressive if that's your nature, you'll speed your trip down the road to success if you exercise some occasional restraint along the way.

Now that we've given you our three primary money-management guidelines, as well as our reasons for following them, there's one lesser (but still important) dollar-handling detail we want to stress one more time—the issue of margin requirements.

Some Specifics on Margin Requirements

Unlike a stock, you can't just call up a broker and buy an option, paying the full price in cash and receiving a certificate. Whether you trade online or in the old-fashioned way, you will have to have an established account with a broker before you can trade in options. If all you want to do is buy puts or calls, you can trade through a basic "cash account." However, if you want to do spreads or other more complex strategies, you must have what is referred to as a "margin account." Basically, having a margin account means you can buy stocks or bonds on credit (or "margin"). *(Note: Under no circumstances can options be bought on margin; they must be paid for in full at the time of purchase.)* With a margin account, you can also borrow funds (or stocks to sell short) from your broker; secure your positions with stocks, bonds or other "marginable securities," as well as cash; and engage in trades with a level of risk larger than the amount of money you have to put up (the "margin requirement").

In order to open a margin account, the SEC requires that you deposit a minimum of $2,000 with your broker. However, many brokers can and do demand higher initial deposits than the SEC-required minimum. In addition, accounts for trading spreads will typically have higher initial deposit requirements, and accounts designated as IRAs may also have different minimums.

Losses can carry the account balance below the opening minimum without penalty, but you must maintain at least $2,000 in equity for the account to remain in good standing. The amount that can be borrowed against securities can vary from broker to broker, but is typically 50 percent for stocks priced at $15 or higher (meaning you must put up 50 percent of the market value to purchase a stock "on margin"). Lower-priced stocks have lower margin values, and neither stocks under $5 a share, nor option contracts, can be purchased on margin—i.e., you have to put up the full value in cash to buy both.

When you turn to the other side of a trade—i.e., selling either stocks or options short—the margin picture gets even more complicated. In the first place, you have to meet both exchange and brokerage "qualification" rules regarding investment experience and net worth before you'll be allowed to engage in short selling. After that, the rules vary by strategy, based on the amount of risk involved. For example, on vertical debit spreads the only margin requirement is the cost to initiate the spread, which is also the maximum risk. By contrast, on "naked" (or uncovered) option sales, the margin requirement is set according to an exchange formula, which requires you to deposit a minimum of "20 percent of the market value of the underlying stock, plus the premium received, plus or minus the amount the option is in or out of the money." In addition, most brokers require as much as $100,000 in account equity before allowing you to do naked option sales—and some also demand margin deposits higher than the exchange minimums.

We're stressing this awareness of margin requirements, here, because few things can disrupt a sound money-management plan faster than an unexpected margin call. Plus, we'd hate to see you enter an online option order and have it rejected because you didn't have sufficient equity to cover the margin requirement. To help you in that respect, some order-entry programs will calculate the margin requirement and display it in a "Margin" field on your screen before you even submit the order. Be aware, however, that these calculations typically reflect the requirement on that specific trade, not the margin status of your entire account.

Let Your Broker's Software Help You

If you use a leading online brokerage firm—one with state-of-the-art technology—your broker's software can also serve as an invaluable tool in the day-to-day implementation of your money-management strategy. However, since we have no way of knowing which online broker you may pick, or exactly how the firm's software may work, we can't give you specifics about the features you might find most useful—nor do we have the space to describe all the possibilities.

What we will do, though, is provide brief descriptions—and illustrations—of the PreferredTrade screens and account reports we find most helpful in the pursuit of our own money-management objectives. Then, if you think similar reports would be useful to you as well, you can look for them when you go shopping for your own online broker.

The money-management screen we check most often during each daily trading session is the "Positions P/L—Detail" report. This display, a sample of which is shown in Figure 6-1 on page 103, lists all current positions for both stocks and options, with today's real-time price, the previous day's closing price and up-to-the-minute profit/loss totals. Then, at the bottom right of the screen, it provides a current profit/loss total for all the open positions in the account. (The only drawback with this screen is that it shows the P&L for the options separately, rather than in strategic combinations, such as spreads. However, this isn't a major problem since

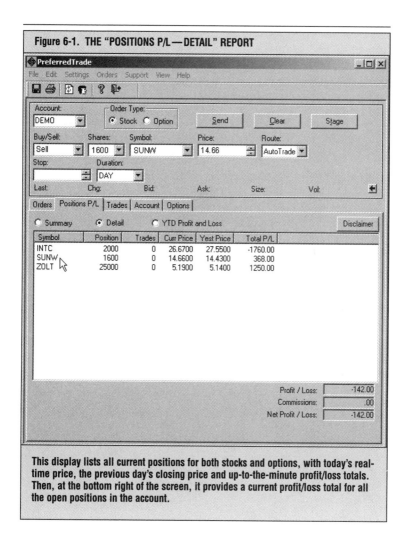

Figure 6-1. THE "POSITIONS P/L—DETAIL" REPORT

This display lists all current positions for both stocks and options, with today's real-time price, the previous day's closing price and up-to-the-minute profit/loss totals. Then, at the bottom right of the screen, it provides a current profit/loss total for all the open positions in the account.

options in spreads have the same underlying asset and are thus listed one right after the other in most instances.)

One of the best features of the PreferredTrade program is that you can enter orders directly from this screen (and others), rather than having to go back to the main order-entry screen. Thus, if you see a stock or option position in this summary you want to close, all you have to do is put the cursor on the symbol, click the right button on your mouse to transfer it to the order-entry screen, click the left mouse button on the type of order you want (e.g., "Sell Close") and click on "Send." That will submit a market order, on which you should get an automatic fill. (If you want to close with a limit order, you have to type in the desired limit price.)

A second screen that's extremely useful—especially on days when we've been actively trading—is the "Trades—Today" summary, shown in Figure 6-2. This screen lists every trade done during the current market session, complete with the price, dollar cost (or credit), the commission and the time of execution. The report helps when you've opened and closed several positions, ensuring you don't forget a trade. It can also provide a warning when you're getting close to your maximum number of positions or committed-equity limit. If you opened a trade earlier and now decide you want to close it, you can also automatically enter the order from this screen by right clicking on the stock or option symbol.

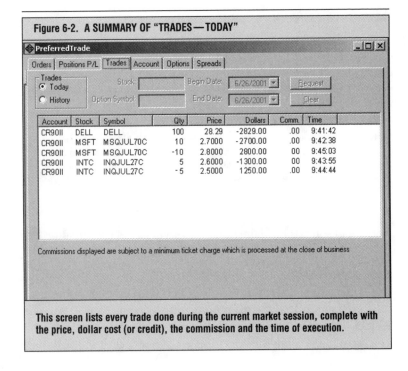

Figure 6-2. A SUMMARY OF "TRADES—TODAY"

Account	Stock	Symbol	Qty	Price	Dollars	Comm.	Time
CR90II	DELL	DELL	100	28.29	-2829.00	.00	9:41:42
CR90II	MSFT	MSQJUL70C	10	2.7000	-2700.00	.00	9:42:38
CR90II	MSFT	MSQJUL70C	-10	2.8000	2800.00	00	9:45:03
CR90II	INTC	INQJUL27C	5	2.6000	-1300.00	00	9:43:55
CR90II	INTC	INQJUL27C	- 5	2.5000	1250.00	.00	9:44:44

Commissions displayed are subject to a minimum ticket charge which is processed at the close of business

This screen lists every trade done during the current market session, complete with the price, dollar cost (or credit), the commission and the time of execution.

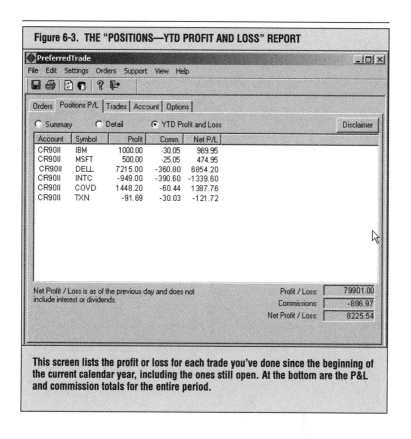

Figure 6-3. THE "POSITIONS—YTD PROFIT AND LOSS" REPORT

This screen lists the profit or loss for each trade you've done since the beginning of the current calendar year, including the ones still open. At the bottom are the P&L and commission totals for the entire period.

Even though it's not that useful on a day-to-day basis, the third screen (see Figure 6-3) we like to look at a lot—especially when we're doing well—is the "Year-to-Date (YTD) Profit and Loss" summary. As its name implies, the report featured here lists the profit or loss for each trade you've done since the beginning of the current calendar year, including the ones still open. However, prices are as of the previous day's close and do not include any new trades opened in the current session. (Also excluded are gains or losses on any securities you've transferred into or out of the account.) At the bottom are the P&L and commission totals for the entire period—in this case, indicating a banner year to date!

Figure 6-4. THE SUMMARY OF "ACCOUNT BALANCES"

Equity:	79901.00	Market Value	21059.00	Date	
Settled Cash Bal:	58841.65	Stock Long:	14129.00		
Unsettled Cash:	0.00	Stock Short:	0.00	Credit Int YTD:	944.88
Trade Date Bal:	58841.65	Options Long:	32285.00	Debit Int YTD:	80.53
		Options Short:	-25355.00	Short Stock Int YTD:	0.00
Available Cash:	69511.30	Mutual Funds:	0.00		
Buying Power:	139022.00	Money Market:	0.00	Dep/With YTD	10000.00
Maintenance Re...	10388.70	Treasuries:	0.00		
Maintenance Call:	0.00	Bonds:	0.00		
Reg T:	0.00			Dividends Recd YTD:	14.37
		Adjustments		Dividends Paid YTD:	0.00
Stock $ Today:	5455.65	Stock $ Previo...	0.00		
Option $ Today:	20887.00	Options $ Prev...	0.00		
Total $ Today:	26342.65	Total $ Previous:	0.00		

The "Account Balances" screen includes current values for both stock holdings and option positions, your total account equity, current margin requirements and your available buying power. Also included are account transactions such as deposits, withdrawals, interest earned or paid, and dividends received.

The next screen (see Figure 6-4) provides the precise details needed to monitor every aspect of your money-management plan. Dubbed the "Account Balances" screen, it includes current values for both stock holdings and option positions, your total account equity, current margin requirements and your available buying power. Miscellaneous account transactions—such as deposits, withdrawals, interest earned or paid and dividends received—are also reported. With the exception of "Stock $ Today," "Option $ Today" and "Total $ Today" figures, all values are based on prices from the prior session's close. Review the many useful features in Figure 6-4.

Another screen we like to look at a lot is shown in Figure 6-5 on page 107. This report—called the "Account Equity Review"—lists the beginning and ending equity in your account each day for the

Figure 6-5. THE "ACCOUNT—EQUITY REVIEW" REPORT

PreferredTrade

Orders | Positions P/L | Trades | Account | Options |

○ Acct Info   ○ Balances   ● Equity Review

Date	Equity Begin	Profit/Loss	Dividends	Interest	Dep. / With.	Equity End
06/18/2001	450479.91	.00	.00	28.05	.00	450507.97
06/15/2001	450445.28	-49.50	.00	84.15	.00	450479.91
06/14/2001	450367.72	49.50	.00	28.04	.00	450445.28
06/13/2001	450399.69	-60.00	.00	28.04	.00	450367.72
06/12/2001	450371.66	.00	.00	28.04	.00	450399.69
06/11/2001	450343.63	.00	.00	28.04	.00	450371.66
06/08/2001	450199.50	60.00	.00	84.11	.00	450343.63
06/07/2001	450081.47	90.00	.00	28.03	.00	450199.50
06/06/2001	550047.19	.00	.00	34.28	-100000.00	450081.47
06/05/2001	550012.94	.00	.00	34.28	.00	550047.19
06/04/2001	550028.13	-49.50	.00	34.27	.00	550012.94
06/01/2001	549925.81	-.50	.00	102.81	.00	550028.13
05/31/2001	549891.56	.00	.00	34.27	.00	549925.81
05/30/2001	549857.31	.00	.00	34.26	.00	549891.56
05/29/2001	549823.06	.00	.00	34.26	.00	549857.31

This report lists the beginning and ending equity in your account each day for the past 20 trading days. Included are net daily profit/loss results for all open trades (after commissions), plus all other possible cash adjustments, such as dividends and interest paid or earned.

past 20 trading days. Included are net daily profit/loss results for all open trades (after commissions), plus all other possible cash adjustments, such as dividends and interest paid or earned. This report doesn't really help that much with your money management—but it provides a wonderful picture of your trading abilities and the overall growth (we hope) of your online investment portfolio.

Although the PreferredTrade software will produce a number of other report screens, the final one we actively use in monitoring how well we're sticking to our money-management guidelines—and achieving our investment objectives—is the "Trades—History" summary (see Figure 6-6 on page 108). This report, which can be quite exhaustive, lets you review every option or stock trade you did during a given period over the course of the past one year-

FIGURE 6-6. THE "TRADES—HISTORY" SUMMARY

PreferredTrade

Orders | Positions P/L | Trades | Account | Options | Spreads

Trades
- ○ Today
- ◉ History

Stock: [   ]   Begin Date: [4/20/1999 ▼]   [Request]

Option Symbol: [   ]   End Date: [6/19/2001 ▼]   [Clear]

Date	Acco...	Stock	Symbol	Qty	Price	Dollars	Type
10/06/2000	C09771	AAPL	AAPL	65	22.3125	-1465.31	Buy
04/17/2000	C09771	MCOM	MCOM	25	28.5000	-712.50	Buy
01/05/2000	C09771	TOY	TOY	-10	13.5625	110.62	Sell
07/08/1999	C09771	MCOM	MCOM	-30	49.7500	1467.45	Sell
05/13/1999	C09771	SGI	SGI	-20	12.2500	219.99	Sell
05/13/1999	C09771	VSNT	VSNT	-39	1.5625	35.93	Sell
05/13/1999	C09771	TOY	TOY	10	22.8125	-253.13	Buy

This screen lets you review every option or stock trade you did during a given period over the course of the past one year-plus—or every trade you did for the full year.

plus—or every trade you did for the full year. All you have to do is specify the dates you want to review, press the "Request" button and the computer will scour your account records, pulling up the data you want. You can see how you played various stocks, what options you traded on them, how many shares or contracts you traded, the exact type of transaction used (e.g., a sell or a delivery against a covered call), the trade price and the dollar amount involved. It's a highly instructive report if you're trying to figure out what went wrong—or exactly what you did right—in a given market environment (identified, of course, with the benefit of hindsight).

With online trading summaries and account reports such as these, it becomes relatively easy to stick to your basic money-management plan—as well as monitoring your trading progress and analyzing your successes and failures. It also means you can spend more time researching the market and looking for new profit opportunities— and less time buried in the drudgery of bookkeeping.

Thus, be sure to look closely for such highly useful position-reporting and account-management software features when you go shopping for an online options broker—which is what we'll discuss next in Key Step No. 7.

Chapter 7

KEY STEP NO. 7:
Use the Right Online Broker

When choosing an online broker for your options trading, there's one primary rule: There is no substitute for options experience.

That's the reason we selected PreferredTrade for our own personal online options account. (It also explains why so many of the examples in this book are illustrated with PreferredTrade screens; it's what we're most familiar with and understand the best.) Sure, there are a number of online firms that that have slightly lower commission rates. And, there are some with software packages that feature a few more bells and whistles. However, there are none that have more experience in options—online or off.

Indeed, the firm was actually founded by professional options traders way back in 1982, when the Internet was merely a futuristic idea in the minds of a few government and academic computer geeks. The company started out as an exclusive service for professional traders, who needed a brokerage to handle executions, exercises and clearing for their option trades. Over time, Preferred expanded to handle a full range of stocks, including OTC issues, but the focus continued to be options. As such, PreferredTrade was in at the beginning when the CBOE and other option exchanges began developing their electronic trading systems, actually advising on some of the most essential features—and they were the first firm to offer online trading services to options professionals. Finally, with the technology available to handle it and the demand sufficient to make it financially feasible, the company started serving retail clients—giving them online access to the markets as well.

Because of this experience, PreferredTrade's online option services are among the best in the business. Their online trading software is topflight; they have solid manual systems in place in the event of technical failures; they continue to be self-clearing, which helps ensure fast, efficient and accurate executions; and they have in-house experts who fully understand every aspect of both the trading process and the art of options investing—which can be invaluable to traders, especially those new to the options markets.

As PreferredTrade founder and Chairman Michael Engmann puts it: "I've been trading since I was 10 years old and I've made every mistake possible. Thus, I can help traders avoid most problems, ensuring they follow prudent guidelines and develop the sense of discipline necessary to succeed."

Make Your Own Choices

Of course, just because we like and use PreferredTrade doesn't mean you will—or that you have to use them. What you do have to do, however, is develop a plan for evaluating the brokers you consider so you'll ensure that the one you finally pick offers the features you want—and definitely need.

Fortunately, putting together such a "shopping list of services" isn't too difficult. We won't say it's "as easy as 1-2-3," but it definitely is "as simple as 1 through 10"—the following ten items being the absolute minimum number of qualifications you should demand in any online options broker you choose.

10 Factors to Review When Choosing an Online Broker

1. **The quality of the trading software.** For online traders, this is the most essential issue, and it takes a number of questions to determine just how many features are included—and how good they are. These include:

- Is the software user friendly—i.e., simple to understand and easy to use?

- Does it come on a disk or can I download it from the Internet?

- Is it difficult to install on my computer? Will I need help?

- Does it require any special equipment or communications features—such as DSL lines, high-speed modems or specialty web browsers—in order to make it function efficiently?

- Does it include sufficient pricing and analytical tools for my needs?

- If not, is it set up to be easily integrated with independent quotation systems and analytical services? If so, are there any special pricing arrangements?

- Is adequate client documentation provided—both printed and online—to help both learn the system and deal with any technical problems?

- Is it attractive to look at—and, if I don't like it, can I change such things as colors or display size? (This may seem trivial, but if you're going to be an active trader, you may be looking at it on and off for six or seven hours a day. Thus, you don't want something you hate on an esthetic basis.)

2. **The ease of order entry and the speed of transmission to the exchange.** This is also important for active traders, who may be placing lots of orders and need the process to be as automatic as possible. Some key questions to ask:

- How many fields on the order-entry screen do I have to fill in to place an order?

- Do I have to actually type in all the information, or will the software import it from the analytical or pricing screens if I want?

- Do I have to manually go to back to the firm's order screen, or can I access it by clicking on the screens provided by integrated trading partners?

- Does the program send the order to the exchange as soon as I submit it, or does it have to be processed somewhere else within the firm first?

- Do I have to specify the exchange where the order is sent, or does the program shop around for the best price and route the order accordingly?

- Do I place orders directly through your software, or do I have to have a browser to access your system?

- Can orders be entered after hours, for execution the following day—or only while the market is open?

- Do you also have a website—and, if so, can I place orders from there as well as through the software?

3. **Quality of service to options traders.** Still another area where you need to ask several essential questions, including:

- Are there separate order screens for stocks and options?

- If not, can the order screen be customized to cater to options traders?

- Are the option quotes provided in the order screen real-time or delayed?

- How about when you call up an option chain; is it a real-time snapshot, or a delayed compilation of last prices? And, is it laid out in an orderly manner, or do you have to hunt for the option you want?

- Does the option-pricing system give you access to current bids and offers, or just last trading prices? How about volume numbers? Open interest?

- Does the system recognize multiple-option strategies, such as spreads, and let you order them as a unit?

- If yes, does it charge a single commission for such orders—or assess fees for each option in the combination?

- Does the system accept stop and stop-limit orders on options? How about stops and buy orders that are contingent on the price of the underlying asset?

- Do any of the integrated quote services specialize in options?

- If so, will their program let me punch in trade parameters and screen for good trading opportunities?

- Does the brokerage firm's program have any similar services to help me with options analysis?

4. **Timely executions and confirmations.** The broker's order-entry program should provide direct access to the electronic trading systems of the appropriate exchanges and, when your trades qualify for automatic execution, report back a confirmation in a matter of seconds—preferably to an area of the order-entry screen where you can immediately see that you got your fill. If the trade doesn't qualify for automatic execution, it should appear in an area on your screen designed to let you monitor your working orders.

5. **Capacity of the system to handle high-volume situations.** The broker's computer system should have sufficient reserve processing-capacity to handle extra-heavy order flow—and the firm should have a system in place to deal with fast-market conditions as effectively as possible. (No firm comes close to being perfect when such situations develop, but they should at least try—not just throw up their hands and say, "Sorry!")

6. **Commission costs.** Many traders would put commissions a lot higher on the list than No. 6, but our thinking is different. To wit: What good are low commissions if you get lousy prices, slow executions and bad (or no) service? Make sure the broker gives you everything you want—and need—and don't worry if it costs a few extra dollars. You'll probably make it up on your trades, anyhow. Do, however, insist that the broker's fees at least be competitive; you want to pay for what you get—not pay to get gouged. Also be sure to ask about potentially tricky items hidden beneath a promise of low commissions—e.g., a commission rate of $1 per option won't do you much good if the firm imposes a $50 minimum on every order.

7. **Customer support.** Gotta have it—preferably by phone, not just online, by e-mail or through a self-help menu on the website (although it's nice to have those alternatives as well). Also, find out whether support is available just during business hours —or worse, only when the market's open. Your objective is to ensure that the support service will be available at the times you're most likely to need help.

8. **Backups for order execution in the event of technical problems.** As we'll discuss in just a minute, there will be times

when things go wrong—even with the best broker and the most wonderful software. If that happens during trading hours, your broker must have a backup system to deal with it. That means having enough phone lines and in-house people to handle customer calls and the sudden surge of offline order flow. After all, no trader who desperately needs to get out of a position 30 minutes before the close wants to dial up his broker and hear a tinny, artificial voice intone: "All agents are currently busy, but your call is important to us. Please stay on the line and a representative will be with you in approximately 45 minutes"—shortly after you've lost your shirt!

9. **Ease of access to account information.** As you saw in Key Step 6, trading proficiency isn't the sole key to success in online options trading—money management is equally important. However, it's hard to manage your money if you can't easily check out the status of your account. With a good broker software program, you should be able to access all key information—including balances, open positions and their values, available equity, total equity, results of recent trades and profit/loss statements (preferably ones you can request by period or on a year-to-date basis). The ideal system will also perform all of the math and most of the accounting functions for you. After all, it's hard to plan new strategies when you're too busy trying to track and record the results of old ones.

10. **Security of personal and financial information.** Many people are afraid of doing anything online because they fear a hacker or someone else will find out too much about them, steal their identities—or, even worse, steal their money. In large part, these fears are irrational—especially within the systems of America's financial services networks, which were designed with security in mind and have special protections in place. Thus, most brokerage systems are as secure as it's currently possible to make them. Still, it never hurts to ask.

Strive for the Perfect Choice

We said the broker shopping process would be "as simple as 1 through 10"—but with all the sub-questions we just listed, it admittedly got a bit more complicated. Still, it's all for your benefit. Obviously, very few firms will be able to give the assurances you want with respect to every one of the concerns just mentioned—but you should strive for perfection. The more things you have to think about regarding the "mechanics" of online trading, the more chances there will be for you to become distracted and stumble as you move along the road to options success.

To that end, review the 10 paragraphs above one more time, and decide what features you absolutely must have—and which you may be able to live without. Then, when the prospective brokerage firm says something isn't available, you'll know instantly if that's enough to make you walk away.

If you're a fairly new trader, you may also want to see if the broker offers any personal, one-on-one investment advice, or suggests trading opportunities to clients. Not many online firms do, but if such things are of interest to you, it doesn't hurt to ask. You may at least get a referral to an affiliated advisory service or information site that can help provide some trading ideas. For example, PreferredTrade offers a service called PreferredTrade Live. (Click on the link to Live Option Brokers on the PreferredTrade website.) This allows a customer to deal with a trained options broker to handle orders and questions. The commission charges are different from the online rates—but the value added by having a live broker will probably be worth the cost if you're just learning the trading ropes.

Of course, the essence of online trading is achieving direct access to the exchanges so you can conduct your transactions exactly like the pros. Thus, you should try to wean yourself from the need for broker assistance before going online—or as quickly as possible thereafter.

Don't Believe Everything You Hear

One final caveat about choosing a broker: Just because the sales agent, new accounts clerk or promotional material says a brokerage firm offers some new software feature or special service doesn't mean that it's actually so. As we all know, marketing people are emissaries of embellishment, preferring to promote the positive and neglect the negative. Thus, the claims you read in a lot of the literature produced by the firms themselves may be sorely over-stated.

In fairness, managers and software developers often tell ad copy-writers that some new service or product feature will be ready by the time the promotion comes out, then fail to meet their own timetables. In addition, sales people are frequently told things that do exist work better than they actually do—and, not being pros and able to judge for themselves, simply pass the exaggerations along.

Our point being: Try to do more than just talk to the brokerage representative. Check out some independent reviews; the popular financial magazines sometimes carry comparisons, as do industry-specific publications such as *Stocks & Commodities* magazine. There are also other books—larger and more comprehensive than this one—that rate brokerage firms. And, you can always do a search on the Internet—where virtually everything is available (if you can only find it).

Finally, before you actually sign the account forms and send in your check, see if you can get the broker to give you the name of a satisfied client or two. Even if the firm picks them, they'll prob-ably tell you the truth, spelling out the things they like and at least mentioning the ones they don't and any problems they've had. If there are lots of the former and not many of the latter, it's likely you've found a winner.

Protect Yourself With a Backup Plan

Be fully aware, however, that no matter how perfect a brokerage firm is painted as being, you'll almost certainly have a problem or two before all is said and done. These could be the result of dis-ruptions at the exchanges, with your broker's computers or com-munications systems, or with your own PC, phone line or Internet connection.

Or, you could even make a costly mistake as the result of stupid calculation errors. Just this morning we logged onto our Internet browser to quickly check the news and opening market indexes—and almost jumped into panic mode when the EarthLink™ start page showed the Dow down 397.85 points only 10 minutes after the opening. Of course, it was just bad math; the Dow was really down just 7.85—but the browser's numbers were wrong *all day*.

Had we acted on those numbers, it could have been a disaster. But that's just the way it is in today's powered-up world, run by computers, facilitated by phone lines and totally dependent on the perfect performance of electrical transmission lines.

To protect yourself from the effects of these technological vagaries, develop a backup plan that goes beyond just expecting to pick up the phone and call your broker when the system goes down. This plan should include:

- Making sure you always have limits and stops in place on your vulnerable positions—both profitable and unprofitable.

- Making sure you fully understand the risks before trying new strategies or initiating unfamiliar plays.

- Printing out daily hard copies of your open positions in case the broker's server fails.

- Closely monitoring your account status, especially your equity balances, and printing hard copies of key account summaries at least weekly.

With those safeguards in place, technical problems may cost you a small loss, but you'll never face a devastating financial setback. And, should the broker suffer a total system failure, your paper copies will eliminate any possibility of disputes regarding your positions and account values.

Concerns such as those just listed are valid, but they're hardly a reason to shy away from online option trading—especially given the ongoing technological improvements. There's now little doubt that online trading will have a bright and very lengthy future—and it's one you should definitely share in.

Chapter 8

SUMMARY/CONCLUSION
Power Up, Plug In—and Profit

Y ou've now had a thorough walk through the seven key steps we feel are essential to success as an online options trader. You've learned how the electronic options markets work, the most effective trading strategies and why it's imperative to choose the proper underlying assets for the techniques you want to employ. You've also seen that good exit strategies are almost as important as finding good trades to enter, that paying attention to the details is essential, and that success is virtually impossible without a good money-management plan—and the discipline to follow it. Finally, you've gotten 10 paragraphs full of vital questions to consider in your search for the best online options broker.

In other words, it's time to power up, plug in—and profit. You have all the information you need to enjoy 24-hour access to the options markets, rapid and automatic execution of your orders and the lowest commissions in the history of options trading. However, to partake of these benefits, you must be willing to face the much larger personal responsibilities that come with direct-access online trading.

You must have the discipline to do your own research, monitor your own positions and keep track of all the details you might have formerly left to your full-service financial firm. You can no longer rely on a broker to watch your positions and call with advice or recommendations. You are now an independent operator

—and, as such, must be *totally responsible* for your own actions. You must also be attentive and ready to respond to both rapid shifts in daily trading patterns and ever-changing longer-term market conditions.

A Dose of Reality to Induce Caution . . .

Lest you think accepting such challenges and exercising such discipline is easy, consider one small cautionary dose of reality. A recent study—"Online Investors: Do the Slow Die First?" by Brad M. Barder and Terrance Odean, published in *Economic Intuition*, Spring 2000—found that:

"Online trading creates an illusion of knowledge that actually gives traders less return on their investments. While online-trader confidence rises with additional information, accuracy does not. As a result, traders are less likely to make a profit on each transaction—and will make less profit on successful transactions. Statistically, online traders:

- Trade 96 percent more frequently than phone-based traders.
- Are twice as speculative online as they are with their offline trades.
- Produce overall returns that lag the market returns by 3.4 to 4.0 percent, even when factoring in the lower commission costs.

"Thus, while full-service commissions can be expensive, they're generally worth it because of the added experience and caution that brokers add to the trading process."

. . . Then a Final Dose of Reassurance

That's a sobering bit of research—and we agree that a certain degree of caution is a good thing. However, we remain convinced that you can be a success as an online options trader. For one thing, the study above was based on stock trading, not options trading—and the efficiency differential between offline and online stock trading is far, far lower than between conventional and electronic options trading. The same is true of commissions—which, until now, have been much higher on a percentage basis for options, than stocks. Instant online access to prices, the availability of improved analytical tools, including screening programs, and the ease of using stops and limit orders also have a significantly more positive impact on option traders than on stock buyers.

In other words, the differences are so substantial that we'll use them as an excuse to repeat the contention we made in the Introduction: "If You Haven't Traded Options Online, You Haven't Really Traded Options."

In addition, the stock traders surveyed by Barder and Odean did-n't have the benefit of the wealth of information you've just read. And we're not through yet! As a final note, we'd like to request one more thing from you. That's a firm commitment on your part to observe the following five dos and don'ts—rules we guarantee will greatly enhance your chances of becoming not only a suc-cessful online options trader, but a successful investor overall. They are:

1. **DO give online option trading a fair chance—at least a full year.** Even if your first three or four trades result in losses, that's no reason to give up and cash in your chips. At that point, you're still learning the intricacies of the online system and hon-ing your market skills. Michael Engmann, founder and chairman of PreferredTrade and a man who's traded literally millions of option contracts over the past 30 years, suggests this strategy: If you start with a few losses, just reduce the size of your trades—e.g., stop ordering 10-contract positions and start ordering five, three or even single options. Keep your size low until you start getting more winners than losers—then revert to bigger posi-tions again. That way, you'll preserve your initial stake and give yourself a chance to correct beginner's mistakes—or, if you're more of a veteran, to ride out your present losing streak.

2. **DON'T spread yourself too thin.** Instead of trying to jump from stock to stock, or index to index, in search of the "hottest" option opportunities, closely follow a limited number of under-lying stocks and only one or two market indexes. Concentrate on following the news and financial numbers on your chosen issues, and you'll soon learn what tends to trigger price moves—and when they're most likely to occur. Then you'll know the best times to initiate the appropriate option trades.

3. **DO have the courage to take a loss.** Not even the most successful option pros make money on every trade, so be willing to get out of a bad position as soon as you recognize it. That's the first step in finding the next great opportunity. And, regardless of what might happen in the market, NEVER move a stop so that you're exposed to a larger loss. That's the first step in ending your online trading career—and ending it badly.

4. **DON'T let success make you over-confident—or even worse, greedy.** Once you build your account equity to a good working level, start moving a portion of your future profits into less-speculative investments. For example, if you start with $20,000 or less, keep 100 percent of your profits working until you build your equity to $50,000. Then start moving at least 25 percent of your trading profits into more secure investments, letting 75 percent continue working—until you reach $100,000. Then put 50 percent of new profits aside for more conservative pursuits. If you feel compelled to keep 100 percent of your profits working all the time, you'll almost certainly wind up being over-exposed to risk—meaning one quick string of bad trades could erase all your earlier gains.

5. **DO take full advantage of what you've learned in this book. Start shopping for your own online broker and options trading program today!**

Trading
Resource
Guide

▲ ▲ ▲ ▲ ▲ ▲

TOOLS FOR SUCCESS
IN TRADING

SUGGESTED READING LIST

McMillan On Options

by Lawrence G. McMillan

Almost 600 pages from the world's leading expert on options gives a complete game plan for trading options. Here are McMillan's greatest strategies complete with precise instructions on how and when to use them. It's the definitive source for profitable option players.

570pp $69.95   Item #T145x-2678

The Option Advisor

by Bernie Schaeffer

This renowned options expert reveals the proven wealth-building techniques for selecting the right stocks, assessing risk, managing your options portfolio and—most importantly—for reading market timing indicators. In terms everyone can understand he provides solid ideas on how to use options effectively for conservative and aggressive traders.

316pp $59.95   Item #T145x-5390

The New Options Advantage

by David Caplan

Caplan presents proven strategies that can give you an edge in any market. Read about a no-loss, cost-free hedging method to protect profits, how to recognize and use under/over valued options, how to prevent the most common causes of loss.

245pp $45.00   Item #T145x-2861

Options as a Strategic Investment, 3rd Edition

by Lawrence G. McMillan

It's the top selling options book of all time. Over 800 pages of exhaustive coverage on every aspect of trading options. Called "the single most important options reference available," this mammoth work teaches you to: track volatility and the key role it plays for traders; learn rules for entering/exiting trades at optimal levels, build a successful trading plan. Plus, must-read sections on LEAPS, CAPS, PERCS and cutting edge risk abatement techniques.

884 pp $49.95   Item #T145x-2836

Options for the Stock Investor

by James B. Bittman

Explains how to use stock options safely and effectively, and how to integrate options into a long-term investment program. Learn time-proven strategies that add value to any investor's portfolio and tactics for investors with varying risk tolerances and goals. Topics include: basic option strategies, understanding price behavior, selling options on the stocks you own and using options to achieve long-term goals.

225pp $29.95   Item #T145x-2419

Options Essential Concepts & Strategies, 2nd Edition,

by Options Institute

Expert advice from the "mecca" of options education, the CBOE's Option Institute. Each chapter focuses on a different essential for trading options. Part 1 covers option basics—what they are, how they're priced, how to trade them and pick a strategy. Part 2 contains practical advice for building a trading system—plus when to buy, sell and time trades, and applying the right strategy to current market conditions. The final section, "Real Time Applications" shows how to apply specific indicators to real world case studies.

402pp $55.00   Item #T145x-2892

The Complete Option Player, 3rd Edition

by Ken Trester

Perfect for those get into this market with limited capital, minimal risk and the possibility of spectacular profits. Profitable strategies that exploit little known discrepancies in option pricing, and other cutting edge trading methods—at a great price.

432pp $29.95   Item #T145x-2882

Conservative Investor's Guide to Trading Options

by Leroy Gross. Foreword by Larry McMillan

Lots of safe and profitable options strategies for conservative investors. Plus, a full section of aggressive strategies for those willing to take slightly bigger risks. With a new introduction by options guru Larry McMillan, you'll find safe, low risk options methods along with ways to use options as a hedging tool. A great buy.

200pp $34.95   Item #T145x-10267

Getting Started in Options, 3rd Edition

by Michael Thomsett

This newly updated primer "Demystifies options for the individual investor." Great reference source for pros, and a hands-on starting point for new traders.

291pp $19.95   Item #T145x-5691

▲ ▲ ▲ ▲ ▲ ▲

Many of these book,s along with hundreds of others, are available at a discount from Traders' Library.
To place an order, or find out more, visit us at

www.traderslibrary.com

or call us at

1-800-272-2855 ext T145

How I Trade Options

by Jon Najarian

Finally—top Market Maker Jon Najarian reveals his private methods for trading to win. You'll find: amazing options trading techniques, proven methods for handling volatility, tips for trading like a pro by exercising strict discipline, and beating risk and reaping big rewards. Also included are easy explanations of puts, calls, spreads and more.

240pp $29.95   Item #T145x-11651

The New Options Market, 4th Edition

by Max Ansbacher

If you're looking to get involved in the excitement, challenge, profit, and diversity that options provide, then this is the book for you! *The New Options Market* contains everything you'll need to know to start a profitable investment program in this increasingly popular market.

320pp $39.95   Item #T145x-11397

Trade Options Online

by George A. Fontanills

This new book from best-selling author George Fontanills, provides online-specific options trading strategies—from the simple to the more complex. It also includes background on exchange listed options, stock fundamentals, and investment criteria.

368pp $29.95   Item #T145x-10699

Trading Index Options

by James Bittman

The CBOE's Bittman outlines proven techniques—minus all the theory and math! New book/disk combo features the basics of index options, including spreads, how to match strategy with forecasts, alternatives for losing positions, price behavior and volatility—and more! Gain an intuitive approach to strategy selection—from an industry leader.

250pp $34.95   Item #T145x-2300

VIDEO TRAINING COURSES FOR OPTIONS

Larry McMillan's Option Strategies Course
with Larry McMillan

6-hour VHS Video Workshop (PAL version available)

Even if you've read McMillan's 2 bestselling options books, there's something missing: The private strategies and insights of the legendary trader himself. Now, you'll be glued to your seat as Larry shows you how to use options to win 70%, 80%, even 90% of your trades.

Starts with the basics and a few simple definitions, and quickly moves on to using options volume to pinpoint profitable buy/sell signals. Then discusses three of his favorite options trading systems. He even reveals every detail of his hugely successful strategies. This world class expert shows you how to sell options creatively, use stops to cut potential losses, employ spreads and LEAPS, and much, much more.

$329.00   Item #T145x-10329

▲ ▲ ▲ ▲ ▲ ▲

High Impact Options Trading:
Option Profits through Superior Stock Selection with Price Headley

90-minute VHS Video (PAL version available)

When it comes to powerhouse options strategies, Price Headley of BigTrends.com is an industry leader, and his new workshop provides a hands-on overview of the top options strategies.

Traders will learn to:

1. Target the best stocks and leverage them with options,

2. Spot trends before the crowd does,

3. Use a powerful indicator—Acceleration Bands—to find upcoming buying surges and pinpoint trend changes.

And, discover the awesome power of market-timing indicators like the put/call ratio. Great for improving marketing timing & general trading skills.

$64.95   Item #T145x-11837

Ken Trester's Complete Option Trading System

16-hour VHS Video Course (PAL version available)

Learn at your own pace, in the comfort of your own home or office. In Trester's 20 years of experience teaching and trading options successfully, he's developed a "Formula for Profit." Now you can learn his secret "commandments" for options success. They take just a few hours per week to trade, and, what's more you can trade with as little as $500. This comprehensive 16 hour video course reveals tactics, strategies and profit-packed secrets. A 312 page course manual walks you through each step of the process.

*~~$427.00~~ **NOW $195**   Item #T145x-9195*

▲ ▲ ▲ ▲ ▲ ▲

To place an order, or find out more, visit us at

www.traderslibrary.com
or call us at **1-800-272-2855** ext.T145

OPTIONS SOFTWARE

OptionVue 5

FREE 30-Day Trial & 2 FREE Bonuses

Install the comprehensive, versatile, complete and easy-to-use *OptionVue 5* today and start a potential profitable trading career!

SPECIAL TRIAL OFFER INCLUDES . . .
- Unlimited quotes for 30 days
- Background Data Base (6-year volatility charts, margin requirements, dividend information, current strike and expiration patterns on all assets-including LEAPS)
- 60 minutes of technical support including a personal "walk-through" of the program—at YOUR convenience

$95 VALUE Free with 30 days of OptionVue 5

PLUS . . . 2 FREE Bonuses:
Option Essentials Video, a $29.95 value and *The Option Advisor*, a $65 value

Comprehensive, Versatile—and Easy to Use!

It's the most comprehensive option analysis available for the personal computer—easy-to-use for novice and experienced traders alike. Buy or sell puts, write covered calls, straddle, strangle, roll out, roll up, and do it all with ease using *OptionVue 5*.

With *OptionVue 5* You Can:
- Analyze any option type—with amazing speed and accuracy
- Get unparalleled real-time performance
- Find money-making opportunities . . . and potentially profitable trades
- Avoid costly mistakes by testing unlimited options strategies in the Matrix Create your own asset files . . . with extensive Background Database and 6 years of historic and implied volatility charts
- Track your own option portfolio-keeping up-to-the-minute track of your total trading account. It even delivers year-end tax reports and more!

IT'S THE SIMPLEST WAY TO WIN BIGGER TRADES! The 2 free bonuses alone cover the cost of this 30-day trial and, $49 is applied to the cost of the permanent program—so there's NOTHING TO LOSE! **Install *OptionVue 5* and start trading—today!**

System Requirements: Pentium processor or true compatible; 16MB Ram, 800x600 maximum video resolution, Windows 95 or NT4.0 (SP3). **Publisher:** OptionVue Systems International.

$49.00   Item #T145x-10144

Option Master Software for Pricing Options

by Ken Trester & Robert Swanson

At last—an easy to use, award-winning system. Designed to help you determine if a stock, index or commodity option is over or underpriced—thereby putting the odds in your favor when you buy or sell options.

Unlike other option pricing programs, there's no need for expensive database access. Just a few simple entries in Option Master enables you to easily evaluate all options in a series within minutes. It'll also calculate your probability of profit when you buy, sell or enter an options—a great asset when deciding whether to enter an option position. Includes a 3½" disk for Windows, software manual & computer program.

$249   Item #T145x-2876

▲ ▲ ▲ ▲ ▲ ▲

Many of these books along with hundreds of others are
available at a discount from Traders' Library.
To place an order, or find out more, visit us at

www.traderslibrary.com

or call us at **1-800-272-2855 ext. 145**

Free 2-Week Trial Offer for U.S. Residents From Investor's Business Daily:

INVESTOR'S BUSINESS DAILY will provide you with the facts, figures, and objective news analysis you need to succeed.

Investor's Business Daily is formatted for a quick and concise read to help you make informed and profitable decisions.

To take advantage of this free 2-week trial offer, e-mail us at customerservice@traderslibrary.com or visit our website at www.traderslibrary.com where you find other free offers as well.

You can also reach us by calling

1-800-272-2855 ext.145

Important Internet Sites

Traders' Library Bookstore . . . . . . **www.traderslibrary.com**
The #1 source for trading and investment books, videos and
related products.

1010Wallstreet.com **www.1010wallstreet.com**
Sophisticated facts and ideas from experienced pros. Includes
volatility data, put/call ratios and much more!

Beyond The Bull . . . .**www.beyondthebull.com**
Provides analysis, quotes and commentary in their effort to make
you a better and smarter investor and trader. Includes sections on
trading tools, a training center, technicians corner, plus much
more.

BigTrends.com . . . . **www.bigtrends.com**
Provides stock and option advice with daily education to make
you a better trader.

CBOE . . . . **www.cboe.com**
From the world's leading option exchange comes the premier
portal for option information

Chicago Mercantile Exchange . . . . **www.cme.com**
Market data, live quotes, headlines etc.

Equity Analytics . . . . **www.e-analytics.com**
An excellent educational resource with extensive glossaries for
technical analysis and many other topics including options.

Essex Trading Company . . . . **www.essextrading.com**
For important option software products and much more.

Online Investors Advantage . . . **www.investorstoolbox.com**
Online Investor Toolbox takes the wealth of financial data available online and turns it into useful, easy-to-decipher information
and knowledge that any investor can use to make informed investment decisions. Option strategies.

Option Strategist . . . . **www.optionstrategist.com**
Options trading resources, advice and commentary from Lawrence G. McMillan, best selling author and industry expert.

Optionetics . . . . **www.optionetics.com**
Market updates, most active gainers/losers, market analysis, Index Charts, research, CMS Bond Quotes, resources and market reports.

OptionInvestor.com . . . . **www.optioninvestor.com**
OptionInvestor.com is one of the leading stock option trading & education services on the Internet. As more and more investors turn to options trading, the need to translate news and events into winning options strategies has never been greater.

OptionVue Systems . . . . **www.optionvue.com**
Creator of OptionVue5 software designed for either the beginning or advanced option trader. Gives you the tools and guidance necessary to develop skills and confidence necessary for successful options trading. Lots of free educational information on options trading.

PreferredTrade, Inc. . . . . **www.PreferredTrade.com**
Founded in 1982, PreferredTrade is a leading online direct access stock and option broker. The PreferredTrade online system for option trading includes automatically priced at the best option exchange; ability to select direct access to each option exchange; stop and stop limit option orders; contingent option orders; free real-time option chain with easy click order entry; and online Bull/Bear spreads.

Pristine.com . . . . **www.pristine.com**
Educating tomorrow's trader today. Free services include Chart and Lesson of the week and more.

Toronto Stock Exchange . . . . **www.tse.com**
News services, latest publications, quotes and comments from industry Professionals.

Guess who's using PreferredTrade?

For online options trading, anything else is too slow.

FEATURING:

- Automatically priced at the best option exchange
- Ability to select direct access to each options exchange
- Stop and stop limit options orders
- Contingent option orders

- Stop or contingent option orders based on either price of underlying security or option contract
- Free real-time option chain with easy to click order entry
- Online Bull/Bear spreads

PreferredTrade, Inc.
Member NYSE and other principal exchanges, MRSB, SIPC
667 Mission Street, Suite 400 • San Francisco, CA 94105

Click PreferredTrade.com
Call 1-888-889-9178 ext.100

About the Author

▲ ▲ ▲ ▲ ▲ ▲

LARRY D. SPEARS is an editorial consultant based in Amarillo, Texas. A former editor with *The San Jose Mercury* and *The Los Angeles Times*, Mr. Spears now specializes in the production of financial and investment reports. An active investor and an options trader since 1978, he is the author of *Commodity Options: Spectacular Profits With Limited Risk*. He is also the co-creator and editor of *Hume Group Inc.*'s SuperInvestor Files series; co-author of *Money Magazine*'s "100 Steps to Wealth" series; editor of several stock market advisory letters and author of numerous other investment publications and articles.